# Works in Audio and Music Technology

edited by Axel Berndt

TUDpress
2015

**Impressum / Bibliografische Informationen**

Bibliografische Information der Deutschen Nationalbibliothek
Die Deutsche Nationalbibliothek verzeichnet diese Publikation in der Deutschen Nationalbibliografie; detaillierte bibliografische Daten sind im Internet über http://dnb.d-nb.de abrufbar.

Bibliographic information published by the Deutsche Nationalbibliothek
The Deutsche Nationalbibliothek lists this publication in the Deutsche Nationalbibliografie; detailed bibliographic data are available in the Internet at http://dnb.d-nb.de.

ISBN 978-3-95908-021-7


Verlag der Wissenschaften GmbH
Bergstr. 70 | D-01069 Dresden
Tel.: +49 (351) 47 96 97 20 | Fax: +49 (351) 47 96 08 19
http://www.tudpress.de


Typeset by editor.
Printed in Germany.

## Contributors

Nadia Al-Kassab
Leipzig, Germany

Axel Berndt
Detmold, Germany

Tilo Hähnel
Weimar, Germany

Robert Harald Lorenz
Dresden, Germany

Maxim Müller
Dresden, Germany

Felix Schönfeld
Dresden, Germany

Hendrik Schuster
Dresden, Germany

## Reviewers

Georg Essl
University of Michigan, Ann Arbor, MI USA

Mark Grimshaw
Aalborg University, Aalborg, Denmark

Daniel Hug
University of Applied Sciences and Arts Northwestern Switzerland, Brugg-Windisch, Switzerland
Zurich University of the Arts, Zurich, Switzerland

Stefania Serafin
Aalborg University Copenhagen, Denmark

## Proofreaders

Anne-Katrin Helmuth and Antje Schuster
Dresden, Germany

# Contents

# Foreword

Over the past years, I have been involved in a series of projects, above all in the field of audio and music technology. I cooperated with colleagues and supervised students. Together, we developed tools for musicology and music education, algorithms for interactive music composition, sound-based navigation techniques, novel sound synthesis approaches, and new musical interfaces.

A common element of all these projects was the interactive momentum. Today, in the era of interactive media we are no longer content with the mere reproduction of sounds and music. We want to interact with them, utilize them, become creative and produce music with them. We want them to enrich our everyday life. Each chapter of this book finds its own approach to interaction with sound and music. Together they address a whole range of different application scenarios from auditory displays over music-making to music research.

Would I have been able to deal with this large bandwidth of topics without such excellent collaborators? I doubt it. Consequently, this book, a selection of some of the best and most inspiring of these works, is a collaborative work, too. It gives an impression of our research and development activities in this multifarious, fascinating field of sound and music interaction and may motivate others to follow, pick up some of the ideas presented and become inspired to develop new ideas.

**Acknowledgements** I like to thank all authors, dear colleagues and students, for the wonderful collaboration not only on this book but rather on the projects of which it reports. I am thankful of the work that the reviewers and proofreaders contributed. Their invaluable feedback on content and form helped me and my fellow authors drawing up our texts and preparing an exciting compilation of works. This book would, however, not even exist without Rainer Groh, professor of media design at Technische Universität Dresden, who deserves my heartfelt thanks. Once I told him of a vague idea to bundle a selection of the most interesting projects I had over the years (some as member of his group) into an edited volume, he was immediately enthusiastic and massively supportive to the realization of this publication.

Axel Berndt
CeMFI Center of Music and Film Informatics, Detmold, Germany
August 13, 2015

# Preface

Johannes Gutenberg's invention of the movable type in the fifteenth century was a groundbreaking event. The new cultural technique led to both, the elementarization of "textual modules" and to the formalization of textual structures. Ultimately, computer programs, too, can be regarded as formalized texts for the execution of algorithms and, hence, Gutenberg's achievement as an integral step towards digitization and all its consequences. Indeed soon afterwards, at the beginning of the sixteenth century, the movable music type has been invented and enabled variable music printing in large quantities. Mensural notation emerged where the note symbols appear and act in a measurable relation to each other.

The first computer programs were text processing programs. The structural relationship between text and music notation facilitated the genesis of music software almost at the same moment, in the 1950s. Hence, music production became a domain of computer applications long before computer graphics and image processing. Although music software development is an important field within the information technology sector, audio and music informatics lead a niche existence at universities and research institutes.

Thankfully, Axel Berndt, member of the faculty of computer science at Technische Universität Dresden from 2012 to 2015, has set himself the task of changing this situation co-working with colleagues. The present volume constitutes an appreciated result of these efforts. The compiled research and study results, concepts, and development reports present audio and music informatics as a research domain that aims at more than the persistent acoustic exposure of public spaces with electronic music. By contrast, it is a highly interdisciplinary domain for engineers, humanists and artists, a course leading from auditory display research over new musical interfaces to studies and tools for musicology and music education. I wish this volume an accordingly large audience that captures the presented thoughts and ideas and develops them further.

Rainer Groh
Technische Universität Dresden, Dresden, Germany

Robert Harald Lorenz, Hendrik Schuster Chapter 1

# Auditory Pointers

**Abstract** Auditory displays, where the aim is to use the human auditory perception as an information channel, are utilized as navigation aids with increasing frequency. With their help it is not only possible to support but to extend their visual counterpart. This chapter investigates how sounds can be used to guide the listener and provide navigational cues in virtual, as well as in physical environments. We call such sounds *auditory pointers* in analogy to the concept of visual pointers. At first we will give a brief overview of different *sonification* techniques and we will review important articles dealing with navigation through sound. While previous work mainly focused on the spatial localization property of sounds, we would like to complement this by using properties of the sound itself. The distance and direction to a target point can be sonified with the help of volume level, timbre or reverb. Therefore, we introduce an exemplary implementation of respective sound synthesis techniques. In two experiments we investigated and compared the effectiveness of different properties. The findings reveal big differences between the sound parameters. Timbre, pitch and tempo proved to be very efficient in contrast to volume, reverb and stereo panning. Finally we suggest to scrutinize the design process of an auditory display right at the beginning and give advice for functional sound design. This chapter extends a previous publication by Lorenz, Berndt & Groh (2013) and compiles further findings by Lorenz (2013) and Schuster (2013).

## 1.1 Auditory Display Essentials

Sound, speech and music are elementary parts of multimedia. While we are very aware of our visual perception, the auditory elements are often perceived unconsciously. Accordingly, their impact and benefit are often underrated and remain unexhausted. Nevertheless, the sonic representation of data has a long tradition and its importance is well-known (Patterson 1982). As early as in the beginning of the 20th century people used sounds to perceive environmental information, for instance, with the help of a Geiger counter which maps the degree of radioactivity to a tone. Similar to visual displays auditory displays are able to provide perceptible information for the user of a system. Hence, audio can be used as an additional or solely representation of data which are either hard to gather visually or which resides in the myriad of input data undiscovered (Pettey, Bracken, Rubenking, Appley, Brown, Butler, Cline, Coralic, Hargiti & Liou 2008).

In modern media the visual channel is more and more exhausted. For example, while the use of smartphones and navigation systems increases, the size of their visual displays becomes distinctly smaller. In order to compensate the loss of the overview of all modes, conditions and relations abstract data are used for representation. Providing orientation in such circumstances is hardly possible by giving even more visual cues. This is where audio comes into play. While the verbal representation is inconvenient and improper in most cases because of its universal meaning, auditory displays are able to present multiple pieces of information in one acoustical event with the help of different sound attributes. But how do abstract data sound? How does the stock exchange price sound, or the weather of tomorrow or of the last years? How can tones be used to navigate a blind person securely through a city? These are typical questions in the field of auditory displays where the aim is to use the human auditory perception as an additional or exclusive information channel to *sonify* data, information and interactions.

Although sounds have been used for a long time for the interaction with computers, they are more or less pre-recorded or synthesized speech or simple, unalterable supervisory sounds. Although even mobile devices are capable to create sounds in realtime, the potential of modern hardware is not utilized to its full extent. Therefore, it is possible to not only play ready-made sounds but also generate them dynamically to adapt them to the particular situation and to use them as individual assistance for the user. Thus, the user performance can be improved and the mental workload can be reduced (Brewster, Raty & Kortekangas 1996, Walker & Lindsay 2003). However, there are not many guidelines describing which sounds and sound properties are appropriate to solve which kind of task. There is a large body of work about the impact of pitch, volume and the spatial placement. These works also investigate complex sounds, melodies and rhythms for particular applications and requirements. But the design process is strongly limited right from the beginning. Comparative surveys are performed with insufficient numbers of sound parameters. Hence, designers of auditory displays still have to make ad-hoc decisions for both, the processes of selection and the creation of sounds (Pirhonen, Murphy, McAllister & Yu 2006).

The scope and a brief overview over the main possibilities for creating auditory displays are presented below. However, this chapter is limited to non-speech methods, called *sonifications*. They are more flexible in terms of parameterization and thus, their application is more ubiquitous. Additionally, they are competing less with the natural language of humans. Kramer, Walker, Bonebright, Cook, Flowers, Miner & Neuhoff (2010) describe the concept of sonification as a transformation from the data domain to the audio domain as a means to enable communication or interpretation. Hermann (2008) refines the definition by indicating the transformation of complex data to sound as a systematic, objective and reproducible one. Furthermore, Peres, Best, Brock, Shinn-Cunningham, Frauenberger, Hermann, Neuhoff, Nickerson & Stockman (2008) differentiate the process for designing sonifications on three levels:

**The interpretation level** describes how a user interprets the sounds he hears and if it is an analogical or symbolic sonification based on his/her understanding of the context.

**The level of interactivity** explains the possibility for the user to interact with the sonification covering non-interactive to fully interactive design approaches.

**Hybridness** describes the underlying principles of sonification, more precisely, on what sonification is based, reaching from isolated techniques to a complex mixture of different techniques like Auditory Icons, Earcons and Parameter-Mapping Sonification (PMS), which will be described in detail subsequently.

A brief overview of the main sonification techniques to create auditory displays is given in the remainder of this section. The selection follows "The Sonification Handbook" by Hermann, Hunt & Neuhoff (2011), which provides more detailed introductions and discussions of each technique.

**Audification** has been used as a sonification technique for a long time. A popular example is the Geiger counter. This approach interprets the one- or two-dimensional data directly and interprets them as audio samples.

These samples are converted into a time-dependent continuous audio signal. Audification aims at enabling the user to conceive huge amounts of data on a basic level. In doing so, specific characteristics, for instance recurrent patterns in the data, can easily be perceived as spectral features. Because of the sonification's focus on interpreting data like they are, it is necessary to know its meaning. In order to enable the user to understand this meaning, a specific training is required.

**Auditory Icons** are natural, non-verbal sounds and audio signals that imitate sounds which occur in the physical world. They can be classified as analogic as well as symbolic interpretations and they are triggered based on events. Additionally they are based on tones, sounds and noises and therefore pursue the purpose of shaping metaphors (Brazil & Fernström 2011). The creation of widely-known metaphors enables the user to perceive the meaning of the sound easily. The more objective, systematic and reproducible the auditory icon is, the better the user can understand its meaning. One of the most well-known examples is the crumpling paper sound which is generated when moving a file to the recycling bin.

**Earcons** are non-verbal audio signals which represent interactions and information, just like auditory icons. Earcons have a purely symbolic character and are triggered based on events. In contrast to auditory icons earcons do not use analogies from the real world, instead they are based on abstract and purely synthetic sounds. That means a user is not able to recognize an earcon by himself, instead he needs to learn the meaning of the earcon, its usage and contextual appearance.

McGookin & Brewster (2011) categorize earcons as follows: *One-element earcons* are atomic earcons which can sonify only a single event, e.g., the sound signaling an incoming text message on mobile phones. The conjunction of single, atomic earcons creates a *compound earcon*. Through this concatenation specific patterns can be produced. A *transformational earcon* is a specialized form of compound earcons. With the help of an auditory grammar they prescribe a basic model for the sonification. This extends to *hierarchical earcons* which create a set of sonifications with the help of an auditory grammar that in turn was constructed by means of a hierarchic structure.

**Parameter Mapping Sonification** deals with the direct and analogic sonification of multidimensional and multiparameter data sets. It creates adjustable mapping functions to sonify specific parameters. The result is presented as a continuous audio signal which is adaptable to user interaction made at runtime. The use of suitable abstractions allows the sonification of complex and huge data sets in an interpretable way. Designing understandable, consistent and reproducible parameter mapping sonifications proves difficult because of their high amount of possible mapping functions. This often requires a conscientious validation of the developed sonification to prevent unexpected amplification effects when the user causes an error. It can also be helpful to find intuitive metaphors to map sounds on specific parameters.

**Model-based Sonification** is concerned with the user's interaction with a data model or data set. Similar to the parameter mapping sonification a mapping function is created to sonify specific parameters of the data set and present them as a continuous audio signal. The sonification is generated dynamically and adapts to the user's input and therefore to the varying mapping parameters. Contrary to parameter mapping sonifications the model-based sonifications are mainly controlled by user interactions. In order to enable the user to control and perceive the sonification at the same time, several layers of abstraction must be defined. On the one hand an appropriate metaphor for an intuitive data interaction and exploration must be found by using a proper input device. On the other hand there must be a suitable mapping function for sonifications of the available data set. Finally a relation between these layers is needed which allows them to affect the interaction and sonification dynamically.

## 1.2 Navigating with Sounds

The human vision serves the primary sensory perception. The use of a computer program, the navigation in a building or the search for a place in an unknown city seems intuitive with the visual sense. We know that the navigation through a virtual, three-dimensional space is accomplished faster and more precise with a combination of auditory and visual cues (Lokki & Gröhn 2005). Auditory pointers provide directional and distance information and allow us to head towards a target even if we cannot see it. Visual pointers help to identify the target when it comes into sight and qualify for the final approach and accurate aiming (White, Fitzpatrick & McAllister 2008). In such cases audio does not only support our visual sense, but expands it. Information that is not visible become present even without using additional techniques for off-screen visualization.

Moreover, the auditory perception features a better temporal and spectral resolution than its visual counterpart (Eldridge 2006). Indeed, an *audiovisual* navigation aid is surely more performant than a navigation that consists solely of either acoustic or visual pointers. Nonetheless, the direct comparison between the two cues showed that both are equally effective (Gröhn, Lokki & Takala 2005*a*,*b*, Lokki & Gröhn 2005).

Auditory displays as a whole play a big role as an enabling technology for barrier-free human-computer interaction. In particular three-dimensional virtual worlds which are becoming more and more common in education and business would be inaccessible for temporal or inherent visually impaired individuals without auditory cues (White et al. 2008). Hence, auditory pointers are able to improve or make navigation possible in virtual spaces like audio-only games or a highly complex presentation of a molecular structure. Learning the structure of a website or perceiving two-dimensional forms without any visual feedback is important for the everyday use of a computer as well. While Donker, Klante & Gorny (2002) use so-called *hearcons* as auditory anchors throughout a website. Sanchez (2010) subdivided the available space into silent and acoustic spheres with the help of circular lines. Whenever the user hits one of the anchors or approaches a line, a specific acoustic signal is played back. Because of its specific characteristics the user is able to identify the object and therefore explore websites or forms without receiving any visual feedback. Additionally, with the help of metaphors it is possible to enhance the exploration of a space once the user understands it. With a *torch metaphor*, for instance, the input device has a certain sphere of action. All sounds placed within this sphere are activated differently depending on their position and so the volume, for instance, varies according to the distance (Donker et al. 2002). However, sound and in particular auditory displays are not only relevant for audio-only applications but also when the visual channel is overloaded with information or should not be interrupted by additional hints and interface elements. Thus, not only visually handicapped people benefit from auditory cues but also individuals whose visual sense is temporarily affected or distracted, e.g. firefighters searching for persons in a smoke filled room or business people navigating through a city they do not know while talking to a person over their mobile phone.

In either case the task of an auditory display for navigation is twofold. On the one hand the listener should be guided to a specific point, on the other hand existing obstacles and threats in the surrounding area should be determined and overcome. The challenges in handling auditory pointers are the appropriate representation of the virtual or physical environment and the accuracy of localizing the user in the environment (Loomis, Golledge & Klatzky 1998). Constant research in the field of spatial perception of virtual cues has lead to numerous mappings by which (three-dimensional) space can be acoustically represented (Grond & Berger 2011). Anyhow, there are very few, if any, guidelines, rules and metaphors for acoustic navigation or orientation aids. Since similar things are expressed with most different sounds, their symbolism needs to be acquired anew every time (White et al. 2008).

In devices for planning and supporting navigation tasks, spatially arranged synthesized speech is employed almost exclusively these days to provide the user with pointers to targets and objects (Wilson, Walker, Lindsay, Cambias & Dellaert 2007). In contrast, mainly non-verbal pointers qualify for navigation because on the one hand the direction and distance of a speech source is hard to estimate (Tran, Letowski & Abouchacra 2000), and on the other hand a speaking navigation aid can obstruct tasks carried out in a parallel way, such as the communication with others (Walker & Lindsay 2006*a*). Klatzky, Marston, Giudice, Golledge & Loomis (2006) show that non-verbal pointers lead to a better performance in situations in which other tasks are carried out at the same time. The simultaneous rendering of a wider range of information by means of speech is less useful than by non-verbal means. Because of its one-dimensionality it is ambiguous or the duration of the cue has to be sufficiently long (Mowbray 1953).

Alternatives are mainly auditory icons, earcons and parameter mapping sonifications. Moreover, according to Wilson et al. (2007), they are easier to perceive and easier in their application. Different studies have already dealt with the design of auditory navigation pointers (Etter & Specht 2005, Lokki, Gröhn, Savioja & Takala 2000, Lokki & Gröhn 2005, Vazquez-Alvarez, Oakley & Brewster 2011, Walker & Lindsay 2003, 2006*a*,*b*, Wilson et al. 2007). In the course of these studies auditory icons and earcons with different timbres were contrasted. They were presented as spatially localizable sound events, partly with acoustic effects. Whereas Vazquez-Alvarez et al. (2011) and Lokki & Gröhn (2005) used volume changes (the closer, the louder) of the auditory icons, respectively earcons, the latter added pitch modifications and provided sonar-like tempo effects (the closer, the closer in succession the sound is played back) similar to Walker & Lindsay (2006*a*,*b*) to represent the distance of the person to a target. For the depiction of the distance of the listener to the target, volume and pitch were preferred by the test subjects, even though they reacted rather sensitive to discrepancies between real and virtual distance. Broadband sounds (e.g., noise) tend to be more effective in comparison with narrow-band sounds (e.g., a single sinusoid). In contrast, room acoustics tended to be less useful for orientation in the virtual environment. Learning effects could always be observed.

Although, every target point had its precise coordinates it was missed almost every time. Therefore, Walker & Lindsay (2006*b*) installed one and Vazquez-Alvarez et al. (2011) two *capture radii* not of equal size around the target. In the former work the sound was played constantly and the target was marked as found as soon as the test subject stepped into the circle. In contrast, in the latter work the auditory display was silenced outside the outer circle but represented the distance and direction when inside, whilst within the inner circle the sound was played continuously and designated the target. The challenge was then to determine the adequate size of the capture radius. If it was too small, the targets were rarely to be found, if it was too big the subjects supposed the arrival at the target too early or too late, which if the auditory display is used in a real environment can be annoying (target not found) or fatal (step over the target). Walker & Lindsay (2006*b*) found a medium-sized circle of 1.5 meters to be most beneficial. However, the size of the capture radius highly depends on the application and/or the desired aim (speed or accuracy). Additionally, Vazquez-Alvarez et al. (2011) found out that overlapping zones with two simultaneously presented auditory icons could be understood if no spatial audio was used to determine the distance to the target. Auditory displays with more concurrent sounds were found to be distracting.

Recent research in auditory navigation aids mostly concentrate on spatial localization of sounds. Stereo or surround-panorama are used very often to display the direction of the origin of a sound (Loomis et al. 1998, Vazquez-Alvarez et al. 2011, Walker & Lindsay 2006*b*). However, these techniques are not handy in every situation, e.g. the stereo audio output of smartphones is not sufficient enough unless one uses headphones. Interaction with wall-sized screens requires the user to turn and move the body and to leave the acoustical sweet spot. Less effort was put into the investigation of the sound itself. With modern hardware even complex sound synthesis techniques can be run and modified in realtime. The generated sounds can act as a function of the interaction in manifold ways. But to what extent do, e.g., timbral and pitch changes help the user to perceive the distance from a particular point or the direction to head towards it? Is the user moving towards the target or away from it? Can certain sound features, like timbre (Zhao, Plaisant, Shneiderman & Duraiswami 2004), be effectively employed to display the distance and direction from a target to be found?

## 1.3 Technical Design

An *auditory pointer* maps spatial parameters, like distance and direction, onto sonic parameters. Today, this is mainly done with the help of stereo effects, head related transfer functions (HRTF) or other sound spatialization techniques (Walker & Lindsay 2006*a*, Vazquez-Alvarez et al. 2011). However, these methods tend to be inadequate in many real-world scenarios. While stereo and surround panning are not feasible for, e.g., applications in noisy environments and on small speaker setups, sophisticated HRTFs have to be calculated individually for every person (Middlebrooks & Green 1991, Wenzel, Arruda, Kistler & Wightman 1993, Wightman & Kistler 1999). Besides the inconvenience of these methods, one main problem in the design process of auditory displays in general and auditory pointers in particular is the selection of the proper sound attributes or attribute combinations out of the vast number of possibilities. The mapping between spatiality and sound is very important for their viability. Different sound attributes can be used to give an impression of spatiality, e.g. timbre (Zhao et al. 2004). However, there are almost no guidelines available to support the designer in the design process at all.

Additionally, alternatives have to be investigated. Thereby, the comparability between the attributes is a major concern in order to summarize the findings and push their formalization into design guidelines. Few surveys fathomed the efficiency of navigational aids although many problems still remain (Walker & Lindsay 2006*b*). The results presented in this chapter attempt to provide a substantial contribution to close this gap. Therefore a software tool was implemented: a realtime synthesizer that is modulated by the distance between a mouse cursor and a virtual target point, both mapped onto the screen space of a 19 inch display. In the survey (section 1.4), the black screen did only show the mouse cursor but not the target point which the participants then had to find only via listening to the sound. The concept is generic and can also be transferred to other scenarios, e.g. to real-world navigation with a smartphone. Basically, it is a question of scale, whether it is a mouse pointer on a screen or a geo-referenced position in the real world. The distance calculations might then even be reduced to the horizontal axis where the target points into the direction to go. Abstract examples for application scenarios are illustrated by figures 1.1(a) and 1.1(b).

The sound parameters used here are volume, pitch, tempo, tremolo (low frequency amplitude modulation, LFO for short), reverberation time, volume envelope, stereo panning, and timbre (the mixing/lowpass filtering of harmonic

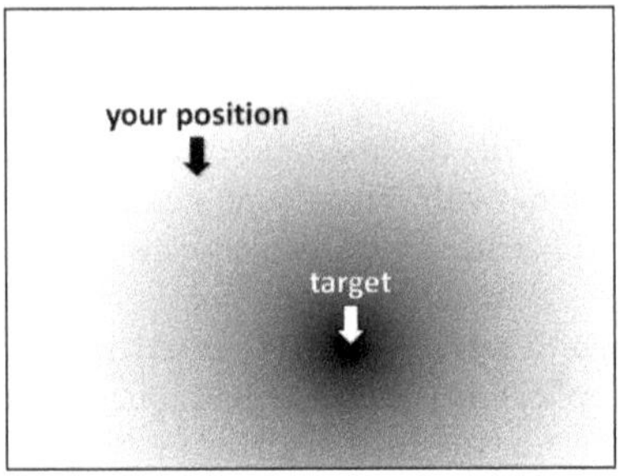


(a) Mapping of sound properties via a two-dimensional scalar field.

(b) Directional mapping of sound properties via a one-dimensional scalar field.

**Figure 1.1:** Abstract application scenarios. The shading maps onto sonic properties like pitch, timbre and volume.

partials and the so-called THX effect for inharmonic spectra). The THX effect derives from the well-known quality label of the Lucas' Films Company and is inspired by their first audiovisual logo, "wings", from 1983.[1] Our THX effect is not a reproduction of the original but synthesizes a timbre consisting of a fundamental frequency and a number of partials. The frequency of the partials is subject to a certain random offset that produces an inharmonic, dissonant sound. The offset gradually gets smaller, the closer the cursor gets to the target until all partials are in a harmonic ratio to the fundamental frequency. The whole sound synthesis patch is shown in figure 1.2 and detailed in the succeeding section.

### 1.3.1 Sound Synthesis

The sound of the auditory pointer is generated via additive sound synthesis. Up to ten sinusoids are added to produce the signal $s_v(t)$. Each of the partials has its frequency in Hertz, amplitude $A_n$ and phase angle $\varphi_n$.

$$s_v(t) = V(\text{Fundamental}(t) + \text{Overtones}(t))$$

with

$$\text{Fundamental}(t) = A_1 \sin(2\pi f t + \varphi_1)$$

$$\text{Overtones}(t) = \sum_{n=2}^{10} A_n \sin\left((n + rand_n)\, 2\pi f t + \varphi_n\right)$$

[1] `http://www.thx.com/consumer/movies/8492259/`, last accessed: June 2015.

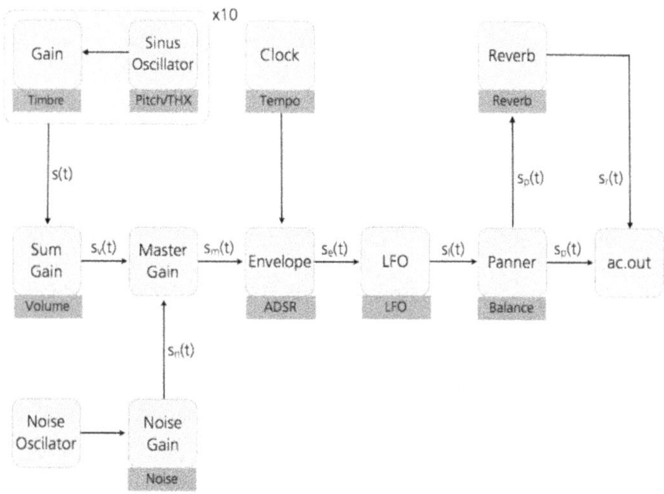


**Figure 1.2:** The synthesis patch of the auditory pointers offers several parameters for modulation depending on the distance to the target.

The fundamental frequency $f$ can be set as a function of distance. If the cursor approaches the target, the frequency of the fundamental and relatively to this also the frequency of the overtones increase and vice versa. This behavior can also be inverted (the further away, the higher the frequency), just like for all further parameters. Parameter $V$ controls the main volume; as a function of distance it fades the sound in, the closer the cursor comes to the target. The parameters $A_{1,\ldots,n}$ are used to control the amplitude balance between the partials. These can also be subject to different distance mappings so that distance changes cause timbral changes (e.g. the closer the brighter).

Normally the frequencies of the overtones are multiple integers of the fundamental with the result that the sound is always harmonic. The THX effect introduces a certain frequency offset to the overtones via nine random numbers $rand_{2,\ldots,10} \in [-1, 1]$ so that the sound becomes disharmonic. If the cursor moves towards the target, the offsets decrease so that the sound becomes most harmonic directly at the target.

In parallel to $s_v(t)$ a white noise signal is generated and added. Contrary to the tonal signal the noise gets louder with decreasing distance to the target. At the

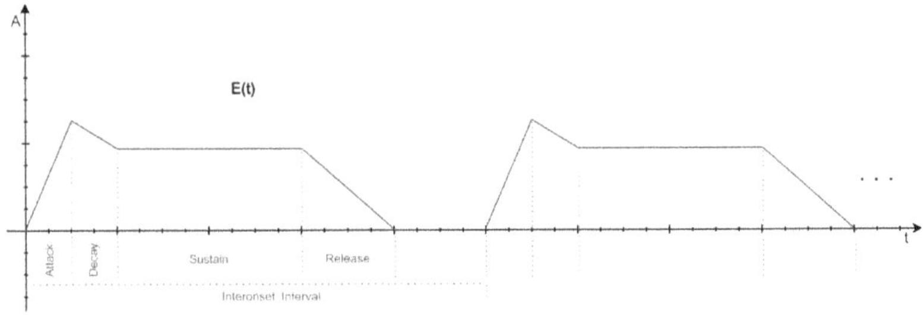


**Figure 1.3:** Envelope E(t) is used to create impulses and modulate their inter-onset interval depending on the distance to the target.

target the volume of the noise is set to the maximum and the tonal sound is at its minimum.

In addition to a continuous playback of the sound, impulses can be rendered and clocked. The onsets are triggered in periodic intervals either with a static tempo or depending on the distance (the closer, the faster). The envelope $E(t)$ of the signal describes the gradient of its amplitude and follows the established ADSR model, see figure 1.3. The length of the attack and the sustain phase can be altered so that swelling or percussive sounds are generated, again connected to the distance. A low frequency oscillator $LFO(t)$ produces a sinusoidal amplitude modulation (tremolo) depending on the distance, too.

$$s_l(t) = LFO(t)E(t)s_m(t)$$

Next, the signal can be panned using intensity stereophony. The center is placed at the horizontal position of the target point. Thus, the signal is being heard on the right side, if the cursor is on the left and vice versa. Finally, the sound is passed to a reverb generator. A long reverberation time creates the impression of big distance; in target proximity little or no reverb is played.

Every effect can be switched on separately, any combination of effects is possible. Interactions between them were avoided in the design of the synthesis approach. If an effect is switched off, the signal is passed through to the next generator.

### 1.3.2 Distance Mapping

Every activated sound parameter is set and updated depending on the distance $d$ between the coordinates of the cursor $(x_{cursor}, y_{cursor})$ and the target

$(x_{target}, y_{target})$. The mapping of distance to the parameters, except for the panning parameter, is calculated via function $v(d)$.

$$v(d) = \left( \frac{d_{max} - d}{d_{max} - d_{min}} \right)^k (v_{near} - v_{far}) + v_{far}$$

with

$$d = \sqrt{(x_{target} - x_{cursor})^2 + (y_{target} - y_{cursor})^2}$$

The variables $v_{near}$ and $v_{far}$ specify the minimum and maximum values of the actual sound parameter, respectively. For example, if the distance of the cursor is greater or equal $d_{max}$, the value of the parameter is set to $v_{far}$. If the distance is no more than $d_{min}$, the value is set to $v_{near}$. The course of the decay graph between $d_{min}$ and $d_{max}$ is described by the power function $\left( \frac{d_{max}-d}{d_{max}-d_{min}} \right)^k$. Its exponent $k$ specifies the manner of the decay of the sound parameter. If $k = 1$ the decay is linear, if $k > 1$ the slope gets steeper in the proximity zone of the target. Hence, the auditory representation of the target is more pithy. In exchange, the radius where the sound or the parameter change is clearly audible gets smaller. For $0 < k < 1$ the behavior is inverse but will no further be considered in the present survey.

## 1.4 Sound Design Study

Usually audio-based navigation research is based on spatialized sound. Most of these effects are based on the use of headphones to achieve the desired results. However, normally a user will not navigate through an unfamiliar area using headphones. Therefore, we think that navigation must be possible with monophonic sounds. The study's goal is to examine the principles for this field of application. In order to do so we investigated the most basic and most widely used sound effects. Nine individual sound parameters were evaluated. The results are measured by objective standards to acquire a high quality and keep the results comparable. Additionally the results should provide the basis for further studies, e.g. with combinations of sound parameters.

### 1.4.1 Study Material

The empirical study was divided into two phases. The first phase covered the parameters volume (VOL), pitch (FRQ), tremolo (LFO) and timbre (TIM). For the latter, i.e. timbre, we used a signal with a fundamental frequency $f$ and nine harmonics $2f$, $3f$, $4f$, $5f$, $6f$, $7f$, $8f$, $9f$, and $10f$. The harmonics fade in gradually when the cursor comes closer to the target, comparable to a lowpass filter that opens in target proximity. The second phase covered the parameters envelope (ADSR), reverb (REV), tempo (TEM), stereo panning (PAN) and the THX effect (THX). The THX effect deals with dissonances in the timbre. It consists of a fundamental frequency $f$ and nine overtones that are initialized at $2f$, $3f$, $4f$, $5f$, $6f$, $7f$, $8f$, $9f$, and $10f$. With increasing distance to the target an increasing offset adds to these initially harmonic overtones, that is what introduces increasing dissonance to the timbre.

Each of the sound parameters was varied by one of the four decay curves described by $k \in \{1, 2, 3, 4\}$. Each of these curves can be described as an exponential function to specify the decay of the sound parameter depending on the distance between cursor and target, cf. function $v(d)$.

### 1.4.2 Empirical Setup

The study took place in a soundproof sound booth that was stocked with a 19 inch monitor with a screen resolution of $1280 \times 800$ pixels, stereo headphones (audio-technica ATH-M40fs) and a laser mouse. A Plexiglas pane separated the study participant from the investigator. The investigator was provided with a computer that contained the appropriate peripheral equipment and also with an audio system in order to observe every study participant's process. The setting and procedure, as well as its questionnaire and the structure of the documents, were exactly the same in both phases of the study.

To avoid a possible influence among the participants we scheduled them in hourly intervals and they were asked to come in separately. At the beginning of the study the investigator assigned a subject number to the participant and his documents. At the same time the investigator presented the participant with a written instruction for the study and a first questionnaire to gather personal information. The participant was told to solve the coming task as efficiently and effectively as possible and was not supplied with a training phase.

The study participant's task was to find an invisible target on the black screen using the visible mouse pointer only by listening to the sounds that were played on the headphones. Through the movements of the mouse the participant affected the audio signal and in this way influenced the sound parameters and their individual sound characteristics. The participant had to get to know the sound parameters in order to perform the "auditory gradient descent" and find the position of the target which marked the global extreme of the sound parameter. With a left-click on the mouse they could confirm their choice, the audio signal was stopped and the exact position of the target was revealed. We set no time limit for the fulfillment of the task. By clicking the button "next" that appeared in the center of the screen the participant started the next test run. For each run the position of the target was randomized so as to compensate learning effects within the study.

The complete study consisted of 180 sub-tests per participant. These were composed of five blocks with twenty runs each in the first phase and four blocks with twenty runs each in the second phase. In each block one of the sound parameters was employed and modified through the four different decay curves specified by $k \in \{1, 2, 3, 4\}$. These four individual gradations of the sound parameter were repeated five times in the same succession. After each block the study participant filled in the corresponding part of the questionnaire which captured the subjective values of the intellectual challenge, the performance, the needed effort, the tension, and the disturbance. The questionnaire, that was used, conforms to NASA Task Load Index[2] and therefore enabled the evaluation of the subjective values that the participants rated on a scale of twenty points which ranged from "totally" to "not at all".

The software program, which was developed for the study, recorded the objective values. Therefore the user's interaction was recorded with a frequency of 10 Hertz and saved in an XML structure. Among other data the current position of the mouse and its distance from the target in that moment were gathered over time so that the whole mouse path could be reconstructed. As soon as the study participant finished a sub-test, the final distance from the target and the total amount of time that was needed to accomplish the sub-test were recorded. Finally, an image file was created which depicted the mouse path during this sub-test. However, this image file was not used in the analysis later on.

### 1.4.3 Objects of Investigation

The examination of various aspects and parameters in the course of the study enabled the evaluation of the individual results, making them comparable. The objects of investigation of the study were the following:

[2] `http://humansystems.arc.nasa.gov/groups/TLX/downloads/TLXScale.pdf`, last accessed: June 2015.

1. Analysis of the objective metrics accuracy, determination and duration which are measured while the participants search the target.

2. Use of different decay curves for one sound parameter. The decay curve exerts an influence on the respective sound parameter's impact as it lets the sound parameter rise and decay to varying degrees.

3. Interview of the individual study participants with the help of a questionnaire. The questions refer to the individual sound parameter after each run and it captures the intellectual challenge, performance, effort, tension, and overall disturbance that the study participant felt because of the sound.

The survey and analysis of the collected information and data make it possible to draw conclusions concerning the usability and stress level which the individual sound parameters caused. Moreover, the variation of the sound parameters through different decay curves allows a more profound examination of the specific variations and their impact related to the objective measures.

### 1.4.4 Study Participants

The study was conducted with the help of 51 voluntary study participants. Some of the participants knew the research field of this study but none of them knew about the exact implementation of the sound parameters that were examined. The following information about the participants was recorded: age, sex, hearing impairment, education, musical training, level of instrumental activity, and knowledge in the field of sound synthesis.

27 participants took part in the first phase of the study. The collected data show that 20 male and 7 female participants with an average age of 30.2 years took part (standard deviation 8.2 years).

In the second phase we had 24 participants. The collected data show that 16 male and 8 female participants with an average age of 28.17 years attended (standard deviation 7.36 years). Three study participants had innate defective hearing and therefore completed the study with a hearing aid device. Another participant was visually impaired and could only complete the study with the instructor's help. His results had to be excluded from the analysis. As a consequence, the study results are based on 50 data sets.

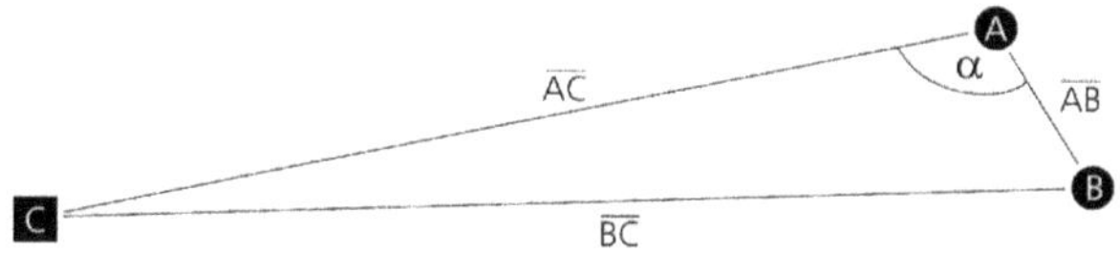


**Figure 1.4:** The directional accuracy is the mean value of angle $\alpha$ between the direction straight towards the target C and the actual direction of mouse movement (two succeeding mouse positions A and B).

### 1.4.5 Findings

We expected that the study's findings differ significantly in the selection of the sound parameter, as well as in the decay graph regarding the duration, distance and the directional accuracy. Therefore, a two-way ANOVA was conducted. The mean values of the examined readings were determined per sound parameter and decay graph over all trials and participants. The mean values for the objective measurements are shown in table 1.1 and in figures 1.5, 1.6 and 1.7 at the end of this chapter (including standard errors). We furthermore expected that the subjective impact on individual participants differs with each individual sound parameter. This might make it possible to classify the mental demand for each sound parameter. Variances of the different decay curves were not analyzed for the subjective measurements.

**Distance:** Mean value in pixel per trial and decay curve, hereafter labeled dist.

**Duration:** Mean value in seconds per trial and decay curve, subsequently labeled dur.

**Directional accuracy:** Mean value in degree per trial and decay curve, subsequently labeled dec.

The directional accuracy shows how the participant is moving in relation to the target direction. For two consecutive mouse positions $A$ and $B$ the directional accuracy is the angle $\alpha$ to the direction towards the target point $C$ (see figure 1.4).

$$\alpha = arccos\left(\frac{b^2 + c^2 - a^2}{2bc}\right) \quad \text{with } a = \overline{AC}, b = \overline{BC}, c = \overline{AB}$$

The smaller the value of $\alpha$, the more the movement is heading towards the target. The directional accuracy of one complete run is the mean angle over the whole mouse path.

| | Volume (VOL) | | | | Pitch (FRQ) | | | |
|---|---|---|---|---|---|---|---|---|
| $k$ | 1 | 2 | 3 | 4 | 1 | 2 | 3 | 4 |
| dist | 142.0 | 93.8 | 80.5 | 60.6 | 79.8 | 68.2 | 53.4 | 49.9 |
| dur | 19.6 | 16.9 | 16.3 | 16.0 | 15.4 | 15.7 | 17.4 | 16.2 |
| dec | 86.8 | 86.3 | 85.3 | 84.2 | 83.1 | 85.4 | 84.8 | 85.1 |
| | Low Frequency Oscillator (LFO) | | | | Timbre (TIM) | | | |
| $k$ | 1 | 2 | 3 | 4 | 1 | 2 | 3 | 4 |
| dist | 171.5 | 110.8 | 96.2 | 77.9 | 71.2 | 54.3 | 42.1 | 40.4 |
| dur | 24.7 | 20.4 | 19.1 | 18.2 | 15.6 | 15.4 | 16.3 | 16.9 |
| dec | 87.2 | 86.9 | 87.3 | 87.0 | 84.1 | 84.1 | 84.3 | 84.7 |
| | Envelope (ADSR) | | | | Reverb (REV) | | | |
| $k$ | 1 | 2 | 3 | 4 | 1 | 2 | 3 | 4 |
| dist | 182.9 | 123.4 | 101.8 | 93.65 | 166.3 | 123.7 | 87.0 | 88.7 |
| dur | 20.0 | 20.2 | 22.0 | 20.7 | 19.8 | 22.4 | 25.1 | 25.8 |
| dec | 88.5 | 88.1 | 88.1 | 88.3 | 85.6 | 87.6 | 89.2 | 89.0 |
| | Tempo (TEM) | | | | Stereo Panning (PAN) | | | |
| $k$ | 1 | 2 | 3 | 4 | 1 | 2 | 3 | 4 |
| dist | 85.7 | 53.6 | 45.3 | 39.5 | 238.1 | 166.8 | 112.8 | 99.2 |
| dur | 14.1 | 16.8 | 18.0 | 19.3 | 12.3 | 11.6 | 10.9 | 9.7 |
| dec | 86.0 | 86.2 | 86.8 | 87.4 | 89.4 | 84.4 | 81.0 | 82.8 |
| | THX Effect (THX) | | | | | | | |
| $k$ | 1 | 2 | 3 | 4 | | | | |
| dist | 455.2 | 370.9 | 354.3 | 316.2 | | | | |
| dur | 19.2 | 20.2 | 20.6 | 22.2 | | | | |
| dec | 91.1 | 90.6 | 90.5 | 89.9 | | | | |

**Table 1.1:** Summary of the study findings. Mean values for distance in pixels (dist), duration in seconds (dur), directional accuracy in degree (dec) for each sound parameter and decay curve ($k$). Smaller values stand for better results.

Strikingly, the results show that the majority of values are decreasing with increasingly steep decay graphs. However, this is dependent on the object of investigation. Furthermore, the results reveal a great disparity between the sound parameters. As seen in tables 1.2 and 1.3 there were main effects for distance, duration and directional accuracy in both phases of the study. TIM, FRQ and TEM proved to be very efficient regarding the objective parameters. In contrast, VOL, LFO, ADSR and REV were rated rather insufficient. Both, THX and PAN turned out to be impracticable. Table 1.2 and 1.3 further show main effects of the

| | Sound Parameters | | Decay Graphs | |
|---|---|---|---|---|
| dist | $F(3,78) = 7.462$ | $p < 0.001$ | $F(3,78) = 53.450$ | $p < 0.001$ |
| dur | $F(3,78) = 4.693$ | $p = 0.005$ | $F(3,78) = 4.772$ | $p = 0.004$ |
| dec | $F(3,78) = 7.173$ | $p < 0.001$ | $F(3,78) = 0.554$ | $p = 0.650$ |

**Table 1.2:** Main effect probabilities for the first phase of the study.

| | Sound Parameters | | Decay Graphs | |
|---|---|---|---|---|
| dist | $F(4,88) = 37.809$ | $p < 0.001$ | $F(3,66) = 33.016$ | $p < 0.001$ |
| dur | $F(4,88) = 8.846$ | $p < 0.001$ | $F(3,66) = 9.281$ | $p < 0.001$ |
| dec | $F(4,88) = 9.462$ | $p < 0.001$ | $F(3,66) = 1.257$ | $p > 0.296$ |

**Table 1.3:** Main effect probabilities for the second phase of the study.

decay graphs for distance and duration but none for directional accuracy. Furthermore, there were interactions between sound parameter and decay graph for distance and duration in both study phases. In contrast to this, phase one of the study revealed an interaction between the sound parameter and transition steepness for the directional accuracy. Differences between the sound parameters are primarily observable with small exponents $k$. Exponential decay graphs lead to a significant improvement of all sound parameters regarding distance and duration. That means, distinct extremes using steeper decay curves can help to locate the target more accurately and more quickly. While the differences between the sound parameters decreased with increasing exponents, TIM, FRQ and TEM always stood out with significantly better values. Concerning the directional accuracy of the mouse paths, there were some differences between the sound parameters, but not between the decay graphs. This implies that the transition steepness has no significant effect on the directional accuracy. Considering the achieved directional accuracy a decay graph with an exponent 2 has proven to be practicable. Using an exponent of 3 and 4 does not lead to significantly better results. This leads us to the assumption that exponents greater than 4 do not produce significantly better results either.

The analysis of the mental workload supports the known results. VOL, LFO and TEM had clearly higher mean values for all questions of the questionnaire (every $p \leq 0.05$) except for the sonic annoyance. As related to the annoyance, the difference between FRQ, TEM and TIM was remarkably high so that pitch was perceived as very annoying. Furthermore, in the study's first phase a correlation between the duration and the annoyance ($p = 0.01$) could be revealed—the

| Factor | Sound Parameter VOL | FRQ | LFO | TIM | ADSR | REV | TEM | PAN | THX |
|---|---|---|---|---|---|---|---|---|---|
| Mental Demand | 10.0 | 8.8 | 11.0 | 9.6 | 10.3 | 9.3 | 8.4 | 9.3 | 12.3 |
| Personal Rating | 10.1 | 8.3 | 10.5 | 9.6 | 10.5 | 12.3 | 13.8 | 8.4 | 6.4 |
| Performance | 12.8 | 10.2 | 13.1 | 10.5 | 11.6 | 10.7 | 9.4 | 11.7 | 13.3 |
| Effort | 9.6 | 7.0 | 10.6 | 6.5 | 9.6 | 5.6 | 5.6 | 10.6 | 14.7 |
| Annoyance | 12.5 | 14.8 | 14.1 | 11.7 | 14.9 | 8.7 | 12.7 | 12.8 | 15.7 |

**Table 1.4:** Summary of the study findings. Mean values of the subjective measurements.

latter was higher, the longer the search for the target took. In summary, no single condition was significant ($p > 0.127; p \geq 0.174$) with the result that one cannot tell which sound led to a longer duration. Contrary to the objective findings, REV was rated very well in the second phase of the study. REV produced the least degree of annoyance and differed significantly from other parameters like FRQ, ADSR, PAN and THX ($p \leq 0.040$). Like REV, TEM was rated with the smallest effort value.

### 1.4.6 Discussion

This section will review several aspects of the study and discuss some drawbacks that resulted from the empirical setup and the gathered results.

**Training phase:** So far, the study contains no training phase. Planning this study we decided against the training phase to tighten the study's time frame and to observe how the sound parameters work ad hoc. The introduction of a training phase could give the participants time to get used to the sound parameters. This may decrease the amount of variance in the results. At the same time the significance or non-significance of the differences can be intensified. Furthermore, a training phase could help to reduce the variance between the participants and reveal undetected significances.

**Calculation of the directional accuracy:** The big values of directional accuracy that materialized during the study result from a special circumstance of the calculation method. As soon as the study participant pauses, i.e. stops moving the mouse, an angle $\alpha = 90^\circ$ per timeframe is included in the calculation. Therefore the participant's directional accuracy will approach the value of $90^\circ$ if the participant takes longer breaks. This may reflect uncertainty as the participant may not know in which direction to move on. But it is unclear, so far, if the exclusion of such pauses may lead to more meaningful results.

**Time limit:** While observing the study participants the investigator noticed that they developed a certain generosity in locating the target as no time limit was set. As a consequence some participants scanned the search space several times in order to identify the target position more precisely; others did not, which impairs the comparability of their results. This effect may be minimized by introducing a time limit which spurs the participants to act.

**Removal of the visual feedback:** In the study the mouse pointer was the only visible element on the black screen. We assume that it affected the participants' actions because it enabled them to use it as a visual guidance. Furthermore it enabled the participants to develop individual search methods and strategies which are already established in visual application domains. The elimination of such visual feedback may give the participants more space for the exploration of the acoustic effect. Additionally many of the participants were guided by the visual image of the mouse cursor and the position of the target that was revealed after each try.

**Different interaction opportunities:** In this study only the mouse was considered as an input device. On closer examination it became apparent that directional accuracy hardly showed any significant differences and is located around $90° \pm 4°$ except for the stereo panning. This can be ascribed to the input method. The mouse is an input device that facilitates the performance of fast movements without much effort and with little strain. The interaction via keystrokes or gestures, let alone walking in geo-referenced environments like parks and whole cities, requires more effort. Therefore it can be assumed that the user is planning his movements more carefully and is more likely to let the sound itself guide him.

**Examination of peripheral influences:** The consideration of more prerequisites such as age disparity, social and ethnic background and education can lead to interesting results. Different groups of participants could be formed and compared. Most obviously musicians and non-musicians could be contrasted.

**Further decay graphs:** We examined four decay graphs for all sound parameters. Based on these results it is possible to adjust the decay graphs specifically to each parameter and analyze their impact regarding the measured values. There is, of course, a variety of further possible decay shape that are potentially interesting, like inverse shapes, logarithmic shapes, cascaded slopes, and more complex combinations of basic shapes. These will be subject to future investigations.

## 1.5 Summary

Sounds are already used in many ways as a unidirectional information channel, e.g. the beeping sounds of a microwave or the output of a Geiger counter. The disadvantage of many such auditory displays is the use of inflexible, static and, often, very simple sounds. A lot of untapped potential for human-computer interfaces lies in the use of adaptive and dynamic sounds. However, there are almost no guidelines or rules for creating appropriate, expressive sounds so that designers are often forced to make ad-hoc decisions and simplify the design process due to time constraints.

Auditory pointers are a typical example of such functional sounds that are already in use in a wide field of auditory displays. Their usefulness is well-known but the representation of objects or target positions in the environment solely with spatialized sound is not always feasible. Thus, the aim of the project presented here is to complement previous research through the investigation of certain sound properties apart from spatialized sound in order to give a proposition about their efficiency and functionality. A software tool was implemented that modulates up to ten parameters of the sound synthesis to indicate the distance and direction of a target.

In a study we investigated the ten properties, volume, pitch, tremolo and timbre in the study's first phase and envelope, reverb, tempo, stereo panning and the THX effect in the study's second phase. Additionally, an alteration of the decay graph was introduced that specifies the sound parameters' distance attenuation. Each of these parameters has been combined with four decay characteristics.

The findings suggest that there is a strong relation between the sound alteration used and the duration to find the target. Moreover the distance between the real target position and the clicked position, as well as the directional accuracy of the mouse path toward the target are strongly interconnected.

As can be seen from the results, the sound parameters tempo, pitch and timbre turned out to be the fittest concerning accuracy and duration. Furthermore the reverb effect was able to prove an average efficiency while the mental workload was low. Contrary to this, the stereo panning and the THX effect seem hardly suitable for navigation tasks. The THX effect that implemented a distance dependent degree of dissonance in a sound caused a very high degree of confusion and annoyance. The stereo panning can be used as an additional variable for different sound parameters and is able to produce positive effects under particular conditions like wearing headphones. The investigation of the transition steepness described by different decay graphs proved to be successful. It has been found that non-linear decay graphs yield significantly better results than linear decay graphs.

The findings indicate that the choice of the sound and the mapping of the distance are two essential aspects for the design of auditory navigation and orientation aids. Even the mental workload could be reduced by an informed and aware design process. Furthermore, aside from a spatial presentation of paths, other sound parameters could be used. The potential lies in the almost innumerable possible combinations of sounds and distance mappings. Timbre could, for instance, be used to find the target roughly in a wide surrounding and, for a precise determination of the target pitch can be used in combination with a larger exponent of the decay graph.

The findings provide important cues for functional sound design. They prove that it is possible to mark invisible or remote objects acoustically without the help of a visual representation and in this way guide the user.

**Acknowledgement** We would like to thank Romy Müller from the Engineering Psychology and Applied Cognitive Research Group at Technische Universität Dresden for her advise in the study preparation, her assistance in the evaluation and we like to thank all participants.

# Bibliography

Brazil, E. & Fernström, M. (2011), Auditory Icons, *in* T. Hermann, A. Hunt & J. G. Neuhoff, eds, 'The Sonification Handbook', COST Office and Logos Verlag Berlin, Bielefeld, Germany, pp. 325–338.

Brewster, S. A., Raty, V.-P. & Kortekangas, A. (1996), Earcons as a Method of Providing Navigational Cues in a Menu Hierarchy, *in* M. A. Sasse, R. J. Cunningham & R. L. Winder, eds, 'Proc. of HCI '96', number XI *in* 'People and Computers', British Computer Society, Springer Verlag, London, UK, pp. 169–183.

Donker, H., Klante, P. & Gorny, P. (2002), The Design of Auditory User Interfaces for Blind Users, *in* 'Proc. of the Second Nordic Conference on Human-Computer Interaction (NordiCHI): Tradition and Transcendence', ACM SIGCHI, Aarhus, Denmark, pp. 149–156.

Eldridge, A. (2006), 'Issues in Auditory Display', *Artificial Life* **12**(2), 259–274.

Etter, R. & Specht, M. (2005), Melodious Walkabout: Implicit Navigation with Contextualized Personal Audio Contents, *in* 'PERVASIVE 2005: The 3rd Int. Conf. on Pervasive Computing', Ludwig-Maximilians-Universität München, Munich, Germany, pp. 43–49.

Gröhn, M., Lokki, T. & Takala, T. (2005*a*), 'Author's comments on Gröhn, Lokki, and Takala, ICAD 2003', *ACM Transactions on Applied Perception* **2**(4), 571–573.

Gröhn, M., Lokki, T. & Takala, T. (2005*b*), 'Comparison of Auditory, Visual, and Audiovisual Navigation in a 3D Space', *ACM Transactions on Applied Perception* **2**(4), 564–570.

Grond, F. & Berger, J. (2011), Parameter Mapping Sonification, *in* T. Hermann, A. Hunt & J. G. Neuhoff, eds, 'The Sonification Handbook', COST Office and Logos Verlag Berlin, Bielefeld, Germany, chapter 15, pp. 363–397.

Hermann, T. (2008), Taxonomy and Definitions for Sonification and Auditory Display, *in* 'Proc. of the 14th Int. Conf. on Auditory Display (ICAD)', IRCAM Centre Pompidou, Int. Community of Auditory Display, Paris, France.

Hermann, T., Hunt, A. & Neuhoff, J. G., eds (2011), *The Sonification Handbook*, COST Office and Logos Verlag Berlin, Bielefeld, Germany.

Klatzky, R. L., Marston, J. R., Giudice, N. A., Golledge, R. G. & Loomis, J. M. (2006), 'Cognitive Load of Navigating Without Vision When Guided by Virtual Sound Versus Spatial Language', *Journal of Experimental Psychology: Applied* **12**(4), 223–232.

Kramer, G., Walker, B., Bonebright, T., Cook, P., Flowers, J., Miner, N. & Neuhoff, J. (2010), Sonification report: Status of the field and research agenda, Technical Report 444, Faculty Publications, Department of Psychology, University of Nebraska–Lincoln, Lincoln, Nebraska, USA. Prepared for the National Science Foundation by members of the International Community for Auditory Display Editorial Committee and Co-Authors.

Lokki, T. & Gröhn, M. (2005), 'Navigation with Auditory Cues in a Virtual Environment', *IEEE MultiMedia* **12**(2), 80–86.

Lokki, T., Gröhn, M., Savioja, L. & Takala, T. (2000), A Case Study of Auditory Navigation in Virtual Acoustic Environments, *in* 'Proc. of the Int. Conf. Auditory Display (ICAD)', Georgia Institute of Technology, Int. Community of Auditory Display, Atlanta, Georgia, USA, pp. 145–150.

Loomis, J. M., Golledge, R. G. & Klatzky, R. L. (1998), 'Navigation System for the Blind: Auditory Display Modes and Guidance', *Presence: Teleoperators and Virtual Environments* **7**(2), 193–203.

Lorenz, R. H. (2013), Design auditorischer Zeiger: Eine Untersuchung zu den Auswirkungen ausgewaehlter Klangparameter auf die Effektivitaet eines akustischen Zeigers, Diploma thesis, Technische Universitaet Dresden, Faculty of Computer Science, Dresden, Germany.

Lorenz, R. H., Berndt, A. & Groh, R. (2013), Designing Auditory Pointers, *in* 'Audio Mostly 2013: 8th Conf. on Interaction with Sound—Sound for Information and Intuition', Interactive Institute/Sonic Studio Piteå, ACM, Piteå, Sweden.

McGookin, D. & Brewster, S. A. (2011), Earcons, *in* T. Hermann, A. Hunt & J. G. Neuhoff, eds, 'The Sonification Handbook', COST Office and Logos Verlag Berlin, Bielefeld, Germany, chapter 14, pp. 339–361.

Middlebrooks, J. C. & Green, D. M. (1991), 'Sound Localization by Human Listeners', *Annual Review of Psychology* **42**(1), 135–159.

Mowbray, G. H. (1953), 'Simultaneous vision and audition: The comprehension of prose passages with varying levels of difficulty', *Journal of Experimental Psychology* **46**(5), 365–372.

Patterson, R. D. (1982), *Guidelines for Auditory Warning Systems on Civil Aircraft*, Civil Aviation Authority, London, UK.

Peres, S. C., Best, V., Brock, D., Shinn-Cunningham, B. G., Frauenberger, C., Hermann, T., Neuhoff, J. G., Nickerson, L. V. & Stockman, T. (2008), Auditory interfaces, *in* P. Kortum, ed., 'HCI Beyond the GUI: Design for Haptic, Speech, Olfactory, and Other Nontraditional Interfaces', Morgan Kaufman Publishers, Elsevier, Burlington, MA, USA, chapter 5, pp. 147–195.

Pettey, G., Bracken, C. C., Rubenking, B., Appley, E., Brown, M., Butler, D., Cline, K., Coralic, Z., Hargiti, J. & Liou, H. (2008), No Vision is Complete without Sound: The Sonification of Telepresence, *in* A. Spagnolli & L. Gamberini, eds, 'Presence 2008: 11th Annual International Workshop on Presence', Int. Society for Presence Research, University of Padua/Human Technology Lab, CLUEP Cooperativa Libraria Universitaria Padova, Padua, Italy, pp. 38–45.

Pirhonen, A., Murphy, E., McAllister, G. & Yu, W. (2006), Non-Speech Sounds as Elements of a Use Scenario: A Semiotic Perspective, *in* 'Proc. of the Int. Conf. on Auditory Display (ICAD)', Int. Community of Auditory Display, London, UK, pp. 134–140.

Sanchez, J. (2010), Identifying and Communicating 2D Shapes using Auditory Feedback, *in* E. Brazil, ed., 'Proc. of the 16th Int. Conf. on Auditory Display (ICAD)', George Washington University, Int. Community of Auditory Display, Washington, DC, USA, pp. 89–95.

Schuster, H. (2013), Erweiterte Untersuchung zum Design auditorischer Zeiger, student research project, Technische Universitaet Dresden, Faculty of Computer Science, Dresden, Germany.

Tran, T. V., Letowski, T. & Abouchacra, K. S. (2000), 'Evaluation of acoustic beacon characteristics for navigation tasks', *Ergonomics* **43**(6), 807–827.

Vazquez-Alvarez, Y., Oakley, I. & Brewster, S. A. (2011), 'Auditory display design for exploration in mobile audio-augmented reality', *Personal and Ubiquitous Computing* **16**(8), 987–999.

Walker, B. N. & Lindsay, J. (2003), Effect of Beacon Sounds on Navigation Performance in a Virtual Reality Environment, *in* 'Proc. of the Int. Conf. on Auditory Display (ICAD)', Boston University, Int. Community of Auditory Display, Boston, MA, USA, pp. 204–207.

Walker, B. N. & Lindsay, J. (2006*a*), The Effect of a Speech Discrimination Task on Navigation in a Virtual Environment, *in* 'Proc. of the Human Factors and Ergonomics Society 50th Annual Meeting', SAGE, San Francisco, CA, USA, pp. 1538–1541.

Walker, B. N. & Lindsay, J. (2006*b*), Navigation Performance With a Virtual Auditory Display: Effects of Beacon Sound, Capture Radius, and Practice, *in* 'Proc. of the Human Factors and Ergonomics Society 50th Annual Meeting', SAGE, San Francisco, CA, USA, pp. 265–278.

Wenzel, E. M., Arruda, M., Kistler, D. J. & Wightman, F. L. (1993), 'Localization using nonindividualized head-related transfer functions', *The Journal of the Acoustical Society of America* **94**(1), 111–123.

White, G. R., Fitzpatrick, G. & McAllister, G. (2008), Toward Accessible 3D Virtual Environments for the Blind and Visually Impaired, *in* 'Proc. of the Int. Conf. on Digital Interactive Media in Entertainment and Arts (DIMEA)', ACM, Athens, Greece, pp. 134–141.

Wightman, F. L. & Kistler, D. J. (1999), 'Resolution of front-back ambiguity in spatial hearing by listener and source movement', *The Journal of the Acoustical Society of America* **105**(5), 2841–2853.

Wilson, J., Walker, B. N., Lindsay, J., Cambias, C. & Dellaert, F. (2007), SWAN: System for Wearable Audio Navigation, *in* '11th IEEE Int. Symposium on Wearable Computers', IEEE, Boston, MA, USA, pp. 91–98.

Zhao, H., Plaisant, C., Shneiderman, B. & Duraiswami, R. (2004), Sonification of Geo-Referenced Data for Auditory Information Seeking: Design Principle and Pilot Study, *in* S. Barrass & V. P., eds, 'Proc. of the 10th Int. Conf. on Auditory Display (ICAD)', Int. Community of Auditory Display, Sydney, Australia.

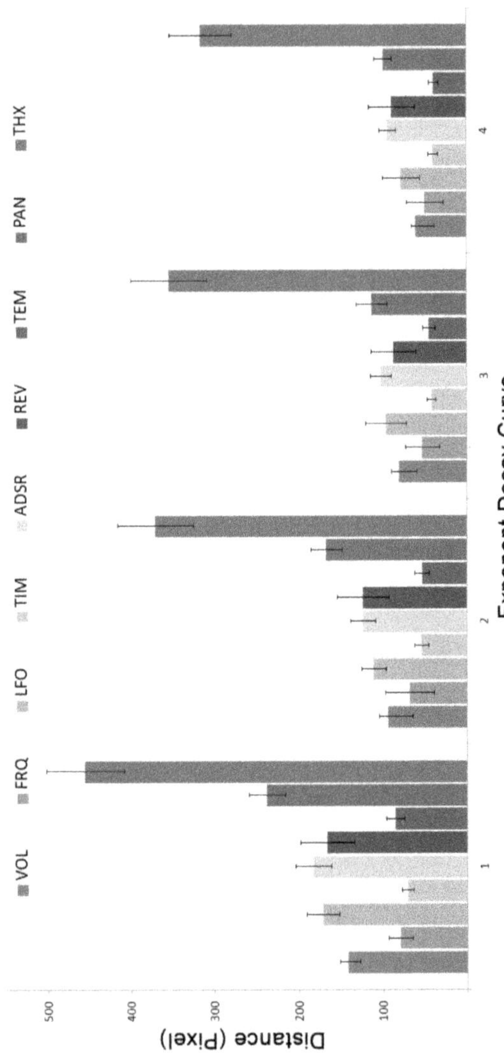


**Figure 1.5:** Summary of Results: mean distance values and standard error of all participants and run.

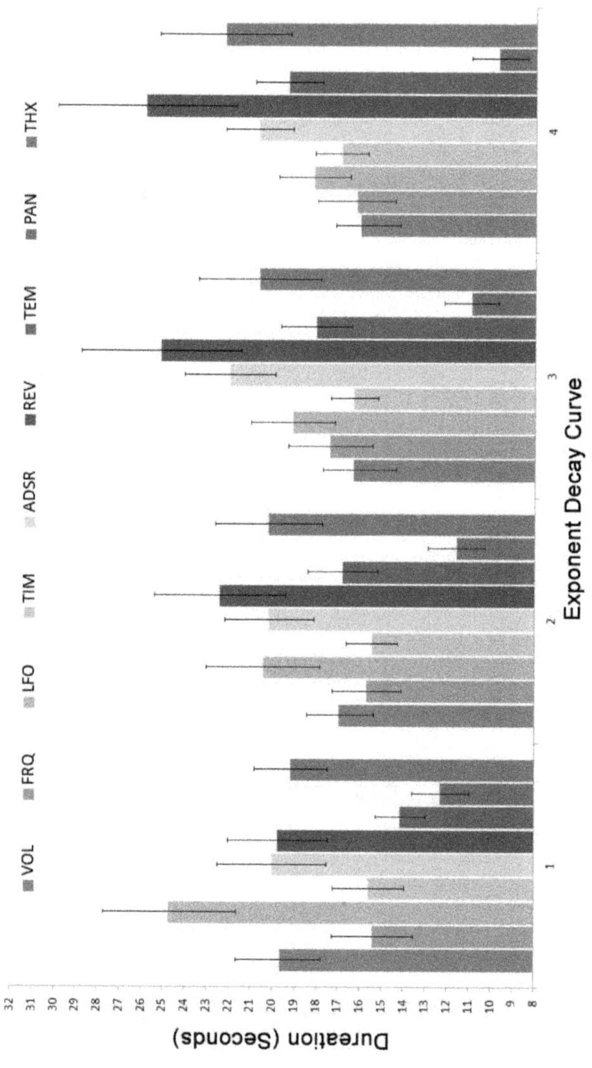


**Figure 1.6:** Summary of Results: mean duration values and standard error of all participants and run.

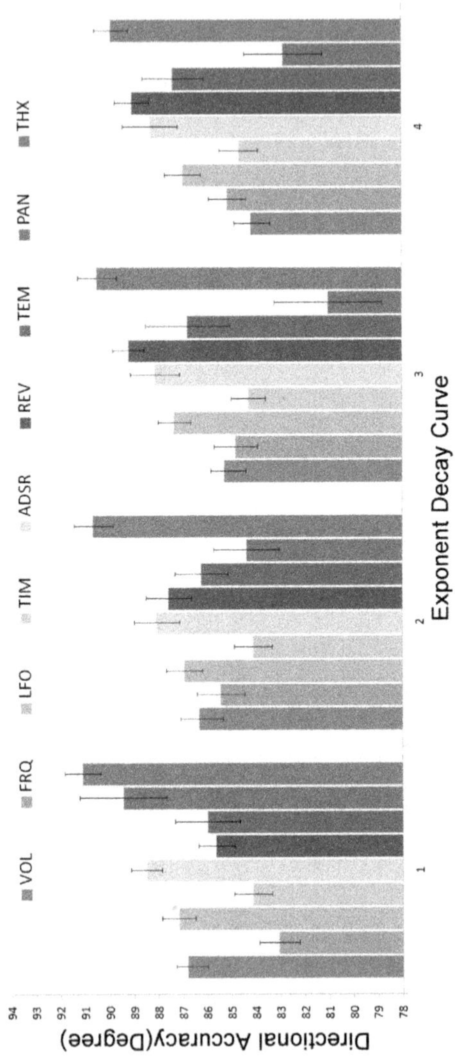


**Figure 1.7:** Summary of Results: mean values and standard error of directional accuracy of all participants and run.

Nadia Al-Kassab, Axel Berndt

Chapter 2

# TouchNoise: A Multitouch Noise Instrument

**Abstract** TouchNoise is a digital musical instrument for noise modulation and is based on a particle system of sine oscillators. The oscillator's parameters are determined by the particle's location within a two-dimensional frequency and stereo panning domain. TouchNoise's sound is created by adding all sine signals. For playing the instrument, an interface was developed, that is controlled by bimanual multitouch gestures. It offers several possibilities of influencing the particle system indirectly and directly. Indirect manipulations include the manipulation of parameters of particle motion and the mapping of particle position on screen into the frequency domain. With the direct interaction, particles can be dragged, accentuated, attracted, and repelled to and from the touches. In addition to these, a series of further functionalities are implemented. This chapter introduces the TouchNoise interface and all its novel possibilities for noise modulation.

## 2.1 Introduction

Realtime sound synthesis paved the way for a new generation of musical instruments, digital musical instruments. Today, these instruments are more relevant than ever. They are present in many musical genres. Conferences are dedicated to new musical instruments and the concepts beyond, such as the annual conference "New Interfaces for Musical Expression" (NIME). Especially in the field of mobile applications, a lot of examples exist with which musical sounds can be created. Their multitouch screens serve as a great basis for novel interface concepts.

Noise is an important element of electronic music. For noise modulation usually filters or granular synthesis methods are used. With TouchNoise, a digital musical instrument that is introduced in this chapter, we want to provide a new approach for interactive noise modulation. The chapter summarizes the work that was previously presented by Al-Kassab (2013, 2014), Berndt, Al-Kassab & Dachselt (2014, 2015). The main idea behind TouchNoise is interaction with a generative process that creates a stochastic sound signal via additive synthesis. The sound synthesis derives from the behavior of a particle system. Each particle is connected to a sine oscillator. A particle's position on screen determines the frequency of the corresponding oscillator and its position in the stereo panorama. Multitouch interaction provides several possibilities for manipulation of the particle system, including direct interactions, such as the attraction of particles to a touch point, and indirect interactions, such as the manipulation of the particles' motion characteristics. A special interface was developed in order to control TouchNoise via bimanual multitouch gestures.

This chapter gives an overview of digital musical instruments that are conceptually related to TouchNoise in section 2.2, followed by a detailed description of TouchNoise itself in section 2.3. Therefore, a first insight into the user interface is given in section 2.3.4. Single control elements are explained with their assigned functionality in further sections. The underlying principle of TouchNoise's sound generation is described in section 2.3.1. Section 2.3.2 outlines the particles' autonomous behaviour and the possibilities of influence. Various opportunities of direct manipulation on the particle system are demonstrated in section 2.3.3. Section 2.3.5 gives an impression of TouchNoise's sonic design space and corresponding playing techniques. Therefore, the effects of the different manipulations are gathered and combinations, sequences or setups are demonstrated. Experiences with TouchNoise are discussed in section 2.4. Section 2.5 summarizes this chapter.

## 2.2 Related Work

Digital musical instruments (DMIs) such as TouchNoise stand out from classical instruments due to the possible independence of sound generation from physical laws. Their sound is rather a result of more or less complex algorithms. Mastering a DMI requires the musician to have basic knowledge of these procedures. An intuitive user interface can help building a mental model of this and to manipulate its parameters. Multitouch screens offer the possibility to build such interfaces. Considering the wide distribution of smartphones, tablets, and multitouch-capable screens the development and reception of multitouch-operated DMIs is growing. Multitouch screens give the opportunity not only for the variable arrangement of operating elements, but also displaying processes of music generation and creation of affordances for interaction. With the direct and bimanual manipulation of objects without the need peripheral devices, they not only feature a better accessibility, but can increase the performance and satisfaction of users. MelodyMorph (Rosenbaum 2011) demonstrates the advantages of the variable arrangement of sound elements on the screen. The application consists of so-called bells. Once a bell is dropped on the playground, it produces a predefined sound when triggered by a touch gesture. This allows an individual and compact setup of notes that would be further away on a traditional instrument, e.g. on a piano, but are arranged one after another, to be played in a musical composition. This can be used as a convenience feature to perform musical passages that are otherwise difficult to play.

Especially in the field of mobile devices a multitude of applications can be found, that are based on autonomous systems, often in the field of ambient music generation, such as the smartphone apps Scape, Bloom, Trope, and Air (Eno & Chilvers 2014, 2011*a*,*b*, O'Neill & Chilvers 2012). Particle systems are a key element of these apps frequently. GenMuBox (Taylor 2012) produces music exclusively by autonomous, non-interactive processes. The whole procedure is visualized by a particle system. The app Love Like Rain (Nash 2013) gives the user a greater degree of participation in sound and music generation. Its interface consists of a grid of white circles of varying sizes. Particles move independently between these circles. In the event of a collision between a particle and a circle, the circle produces a sound derived from its size, and the particle changes direction, i.e. bounces off. Particles are created randomly or by touch gestures. The particle speed is determined by the inclination of the mobile device, and the direction of the particle motion depends on the orientation of the device. Hence, the instrument plays itself but can be influenced by the user. The design of the Kinetic Particle Synthesizer (Kuhara & Kobayashi 2011) features a similar principle. It assigns the sound to the particles. When particles collide with each other or with a range limit, percussive sounds are triggered. These sounds are calculated by the kinetic properties of the particles. Again, the parameters of motion are influenced by tilting the device along an axis. The dynamic sequencer NodeBeat (Sandler & Windl 2013) allows a flexible degree of user participation. The basis of the instrument is formed by a system of generators and node elements, that either move freely over the screen or stay inflexible at a position and that can communicate with each other. First after starting NodeBeat, the user creates some elements and determines various parameters of sound, motion and communication between the nodes and generators. Once a desired setup is prepared or loaded from memory, the user can let the instrument play itself without further involvement and set a sleep timer.

It is also possible to have individual elements in a particle system communicate with each other, and also adapt their behavior to that of other individuals, as in the case of swarm simulations. Here, the individuals are aware of their neighborhood and adjust their motion based on this knowledge. Blackwell & Young (2004) link swarm intelligence with improvised music. They integrate the aural environment into the swarms' neighborhood by forming attractors according to parametrized audio events. In this way, the swarm is able to react to a human performer as well as the human performer reacts to the swarm. Comprehensive studies of the possibilities of using swarm algorithms for music generation were conducted in the context of the Swarms project[1] at the Zurich University of the Arts. In cooperation with collaborators the project lead to a series of installations and performances, that followed the concept and programming environment Interactive Swarm Orchestra (ISO) and the affiliated interaction and projection surface Interactive Swarm Space (ISS). A collection of open source C++ libraries for developing swarm-based music installations emerged from this project. A further outcome of ISO are "guidelines and strategies for creating aesthetically meaningful relationships between swarm behavior and musical structure."[2] FlowSpace (Bisig, Schacher & Neukom 2011) is one of the audiovisual installations that take place in ISO. Visitors can interact with the particle system via a touch sensitive surface. Two pentagonal canvases above serve as a panoramic representation of visual components. The spatialization of the sound is achieved by Ambisonics. There are three different setups implemented in FlowSpace. The eco and music system LUSH (Choi & Wang 2010) generates swarms from MIDI files. For this purpose, it uses the pitch values as parameter for swarm generation. The single individuals enter the screen separately or in flocks in different temporal intervals. So-called playheads are used for interaction with the system. These are lines, which can be drawn on the interface by mouse movement. Collisions of a swarm individual with a playhead are collected by the so-called playque, which plays the node or sends an OSC message. The system allows using up to five playheads and two playques.

The Photophore app (Dika 2014) uses up to 100 swarm individuals that are assigned to sound generators, i.e. oscillators. They create vibrant chorus effects

[1] `http://swarms.cc/`, last accessed: May 2015.

[2] `http://swarms.cc/about/project/`, last accessed: May 2015.

by moving through a three-dimensional environment following a flocking algorithm and physics simulation. The user has various options to manipulate the motion by controlling speed, turbulence, attraction, alignment, and separation from which the chorus parameters derive. Additionally, touches on the playground chase away the individuals. The user can create up to six voices and assign up to six different waveforms to the oscillators. Low- and highpass filters are implemented in Photophore, as well as amplitude and filter envelopes, stereo echo effects and an arpeggiator. The app supports the use of MIDI keyboards and can be connected with other apps via AudioBus and Inter-App Audio or CoreMIDI, respectively. This is a typical example how such instruments are integrated into a bigger Digital Audio Workstation setup.

## 2.3 Concept & Development

The basis of TouchNoise is formed by a particle system, that is displayed on a two dimensional plane on the screen, the so-called playground. Every particle is assigned to a sine oscillator, whose parameters (frequency and stereo position) are determined by the particle position. The vertical axis corresponds to the oscillator's frequency, ranging from 20Hz to 20kHz or user-defined borders in-between. The mapping of the vertical position on the playground onto the oscillators' frequency can be set linear and logarithmic, and can be further customized by pinch gestures on the playground, which creates a more complex non-linear mapping. The horizontal position determines the oscillator's position in the stereo sound field. The current implementation allows up to 200 particles inhabiting the playground. For the final output all sine signals are added. All further descriptions give a rough overview of the functionalities and interactions implemented in TouchNoise, which will be detailed in the subsequent subsections.

Particles can be added to and deleted from the playground either at random positions or at specific touch positions. They can have infinite or finite lifetime. In the latter case, each particle is deleted when the time span expires.

The particles behave according to several motion principles, by default the particles perform a Brownian motion[3] with a certain step width and maximum rotation angle. This behavior creates a stochastic distribution of the particles on the playground and correspondingly inharmonic and noisy output spectra. This

[3] Brownian motion in 2d: rotate by a random angle, make a step forward, rotate by a random angle, make a step forward, and so on.

is the basic sound of TouchNoise. Further principles of particle motion introduce rules for flocking behavior (alignment, separation, and cohesion), following leader particles and movement along a vector field. Each of these principles influences the particle motion and distribution in a certain way (e.g., by creating clusters of particles), which is also reflected in the audio output (e.g., by clusters of sinusoids). The user can adjust how much the particle motion is affected by each principle to create a mixed characteristic.

The previously described manipulations influence the particle system in a mainly indirect way seen from the perspective of interaction. For direct interactions touch gestures can be assigned with several modes of influence. In *magnetic* mode, particles are attracted toward the touch points on the playground. *Repel* mode is the opposite of magnetic mode, it chases the particles away. In *drag* mode, the particles that get under a touch point are attached to it and can be dragged. The volume level of particles under and close to a touch point can be altered in *accentuation* mode. Therefore, TouchNoise defines two different volume levels: the main volume for all particles and the accentuation volume for particles affected by accentuation mode. All these modes can also be assigned to frequency bands, i.e. whole rows in the playground, that divide the frequency domain into discrete areas. Different musical scales can be chosen for this discretization, e.g. a chromatic scale, a pentatonic scale and others. A further mode exclusive to frequency bands is the *quantization* mode. Each particle, that enters a quantized frequency band, plays the corresponding frequency until it leaves the band, instead of a continuous glissando. The interaction modes can be combined to create more complex behaviors. The frequency bands can also be triggered via a MIDI keyboard.

Figure 2.1 gives an overview of the various interactive functions that TouchNoise implements. During the development of TouchNoise we were faced with two major challenges, which will be detailed subsequently: the implementation of a particle system performing the desired functionality, and the design of the user interface itself, including the graphical user interfaces (GUI) and the (partly bimanual) multitouch gestures. The GUI is shown in figure 2.8.

### 2.3.1 Sound Generation

TouchNoise's sound generation is based on additive synthesis, illustrated in figure 2.2. Single sine signals, one for each particle on the playground, are added up to form the output signal. A particle's horizontal position on the playground

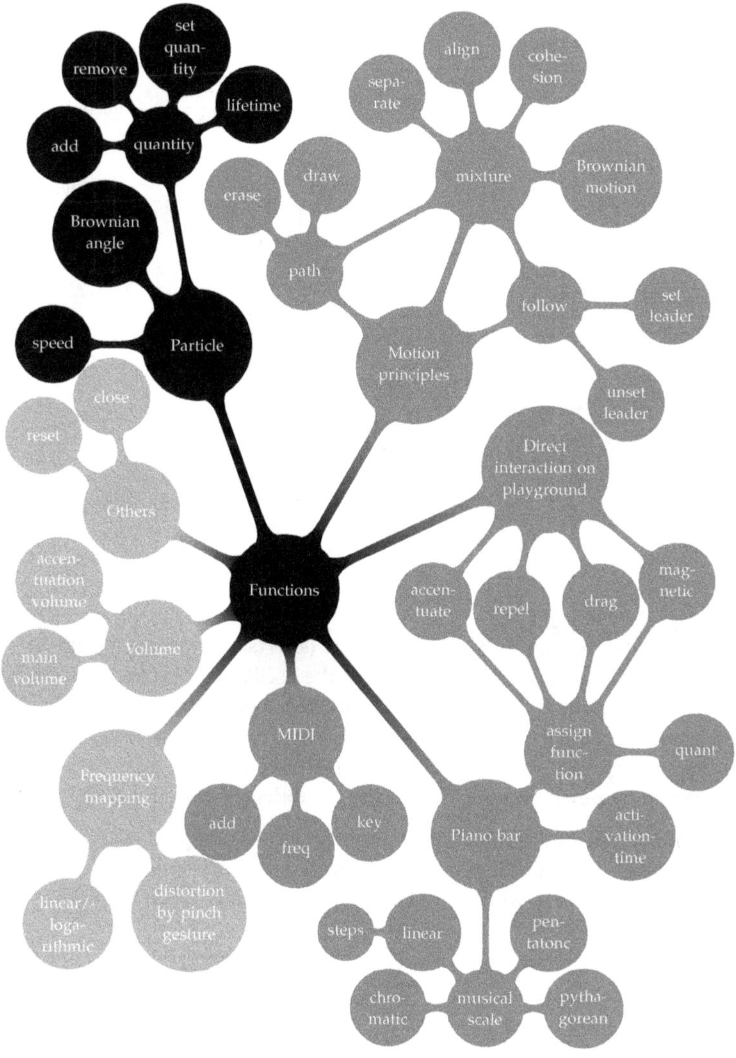


**Figure 2.1:** The functions of TouchNoise. The darker the color the higher is a function's priority within the interaction concept.

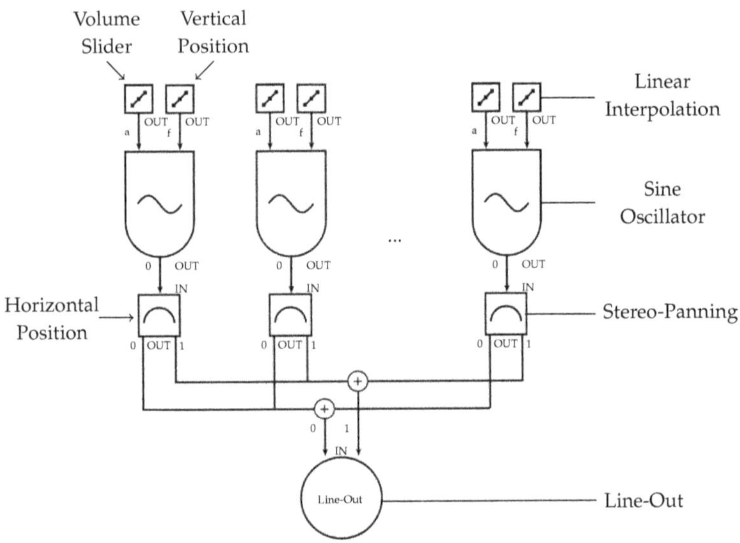


**Figure 2.2:** The sound synthesis of TouchNoise.

determines its position in the stereo sound field (stereo-panning) and its vertical position determines the frequency of the oscillator. The frequency ranges from 20Hz to 20kHz. By default, the relation between the vertical axis of the playground and the frequency domain is linear. This can be turned into a musically more useful logarithmic mapping. User-defined nonlinear mappings can be achieved by pinch gestures on the playground, as shown in figure 2.3.

Each particle passes amplitude and frequency to its assigned oscillator, which generates the corresponding sine signal. In order to prevent discontinuities in the frequency domain, which would cause click sounds when the frequency of

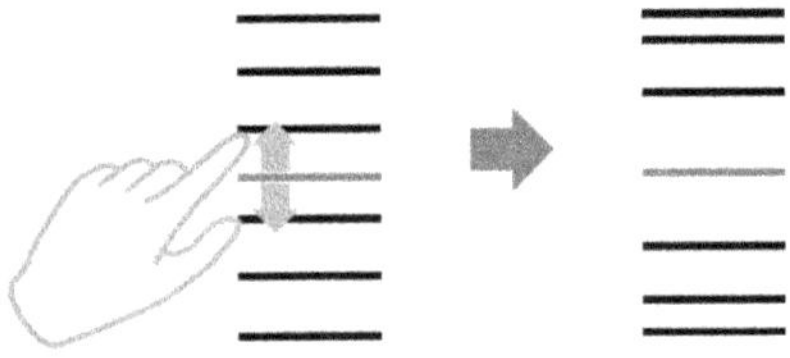

**Figure 2.3:** Nonlinear distortion of the frequency mapping via pinch gesture.

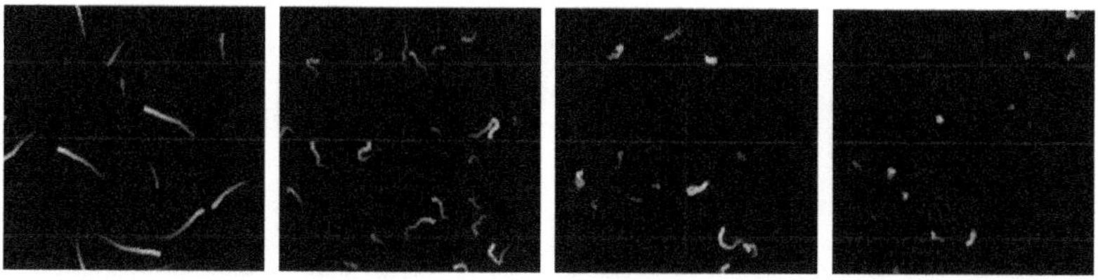

(a) 20° (b) 120° (c) 230° (d) 359°

**Figure 2.4:** Impact of the maximal Brownian angle to the particle motion.

an oscillator changes, we use linear frequency envelopes. Afterwards, a stereo signal is calculated according to the horizontal position of the particle on the playground. All oscillator signals are then added up to form the LineOut signal. For the audio synthesis of TouchNoise we apply the JSyn audio synthesis API[4] in version 16.6.4.

### 2.3.2 Particle Motion

By default the movement of the particles underlies the principle of Brownian motion. Here, a particle rotates by a random angle. Afterwards, the particle makes one step ahead and the procedure repeats itself. This motion characteristic can be further specified by the user through two different parameters, the maximal rotation angle (also called Brownian angle) and the step width. Figure 2.4 displays the effect of different values for the maximum angle to the particle motion. Narrow angles cause straighter particle movement and a more lively noise spectrum. With a wide maximum rotation angle, by contrast, the particles stay closer to their current position, which causes a more static noise spectrum. The second motion parameter, the particle step width, affects the particles' speed. Small steps have a similar effect as a big Brownian angle, i.e. less activity in the sound spectrum, and vice versa.

The frequency range of the particle motion is delimited by an upper and lower border on the playground. These can be shifted by the user. The closer they are placed to each other, the more particles concentrate within an increasingly narrow band, contributing more sound energy to this frequency band.

[4] `http://www.softsynth.com/jsyn/`, last accessed: June 2015.

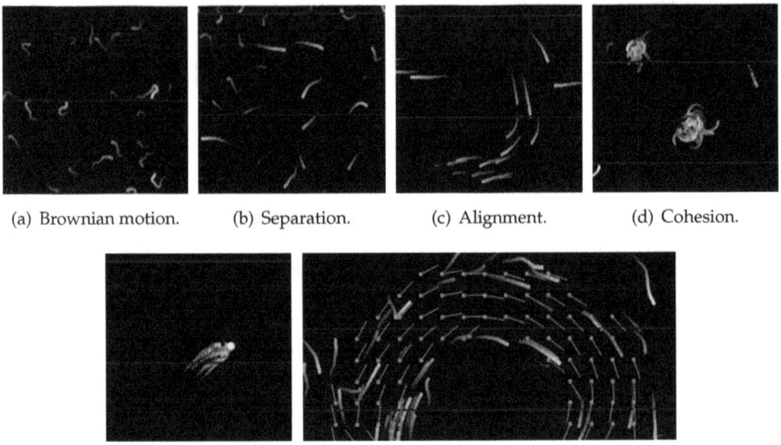

(a) Brownian motion. (b) Separation. (c) Alignment. (d) Cohesion.

(e) Following. (f) Flow field.

**Figure 2.5:** Particle motion according to different behavioral rules.

The mapping of the playground's vertical axis onto the frequency domain can be switched between a linear and a more musical, logarithmic mode, and further distorted by pinch gestures to either compress a wider frequency range into a narrow horizontal band on the playground, or to expand a narrow frequency band over a wider region on the playground. The particles, however, will not adapt the speed at which they travel through the playground. This has the effect that particles remain longer and move slower in expanded frequency bands and move faster in compressed frequency bands. The noise generated here differs from the noise generated with a linear mapping.

So far, it is hard to define longterm behavior in the particle flow. With Brownian motion the particles spread uniformly and create an equal distribution throughout the playground. To enrich this behavior and enable more nuanced characteristics, we added flocking functionalities based on Reynolds' (1987, 2007) Boids algorithm (this includes alignment, separation and cohesion of particles), orientation towards a leader particle (follow), and movement along a user-defined flow field. All characteristics are illustrated in figure 2.5. The effect that each of these rules has on the particle motion can be weighted by the user to create mixed behaviors.

The *alignment* rule causes the particles to adjust their direction to their neighbors' directions. In this way, similar sequences of particle movements evolve, that stand out in the frequency spectrum because of the higher concentration of particles. Particles that follow the *cohesion* rule approximate their positions and head into the center of all particles surrounding them. By this means, particle nests are formed that cause a high representation of few frequencies in the spectrum. Each nest causes a narrow band noise signal at its position in the stereo field. With the *separation* rule a minimum distance between the particles is maintained. This can help to achieve an even distribution of particles throughout the playground, alleviate flocking, and create white noise. According to the *follow* rule, all particles that are in the neighborhood of a leader particle adjust their direction towards the leader particle. The sonic effect is similar to the effect of the *alignment* rule. Before the *follow* rule comes into effect, the user needs to create at least one leader particle by performing a drag gesture on the playground. The initial direction of the new particle is adopted from the direction of the drag gesture. Applying the *flow field* rule, the particles move along a path that the user can draw on the playground by drag gestures. In this way, longterm sequences and patterns can be created.

### 2.3.3 Direct Interaction with the Particle System

The manipulations of the particle motion described so far affect the general behavior of the particle system. This is controlled via certain parameters that are passed over by the user. These parameters are set via certain control elements of the graphical user interface, which is a very indirect way of interacting with the particle system. In addition to this, TouchNoise offers different opportunities for direct interaction: the creation and deletion of particles as well as different modes that influence the particle flow and distribution, which can be assigned to touch gestures and frequency bands.

Particles can be placed on the playground and deleted from it either at random positions or by tap and drag gestures directly on the playground. In the latter case, not only the number but also the initial distribution of the particles is defined by the user. With only a few particles on the playground, the listener can clearly distinguish single sine signals in the spectrum, whereas a large number of particles results in an increasingly dense, noisy sound. Likewise, the more particles cluster around a certain position, the denser is the sound of the cluster. In the current implementation up to 200 particles can be added to the playground. Once created, each particle has a lifetime of at least 100 millisec-

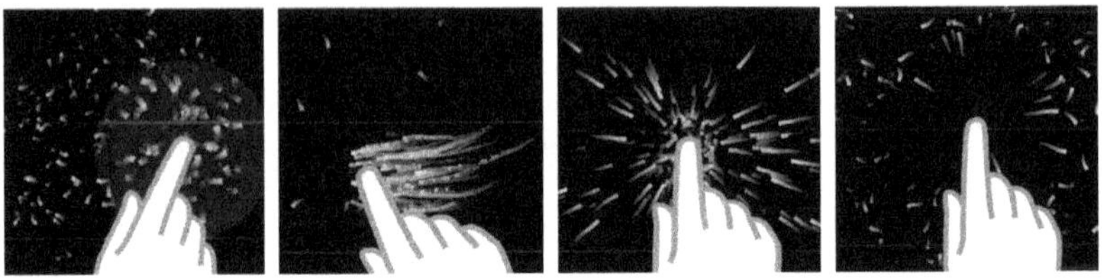

(a) Accentuation mode. (b) Drag mode. (c) Magnetic mode. (d) Repel mode.

**Figure 2.6:** Modes of direct touch interaction with the particles.

onds (this creates chimes-like sound effects). The maximum setting is an infinite lifetime, so that it is the users task to delete the particle.

For direct interaction with the particles on the playground, we implemented several modes: the accentuation mode, drag mode, magnetic mode, and repel mode. The four modes are applied to the playground via one or more touches. Each touch creates a corresponding effect field at and around the touch with an adjustable radius. The influence of each mode on the particle system is illustrated in figure 2.6.

The *accentuation* mode affects the amplitude of particles that are located within the effect range of a touch point. The user can also set the volume level for affected, i.e. accentuated, and non-affected particles. The accentuation level can even be below the general volume level, which causes holes in the spectrum at the corresponding touch positions.

The *drag* mode causes particles, once they get under a touch point, to stick to the touch and follow subsequent drag gestures until the touch is released. With this interaction particles can be collected to form a dense cluster in the frequency spectrum frequencies. In most caeses, a user-driven drag gesture will also feature a different speed compared to unaffected particles, which creates clearly audible sweep sounds.

In *magnetic* mode all particles that are located within the effect range are attracted toward the coordinates of the user's touch. Affected particles head directly for this point. Sonically, the energy of the corresponding region in the stereophonic frequency spectrum shrinks into a dense cluster. When the attractive force is released, the cluster dissolves and fades back to an equipartition over the playground and stereophonic frequency spectrum, respectively. This

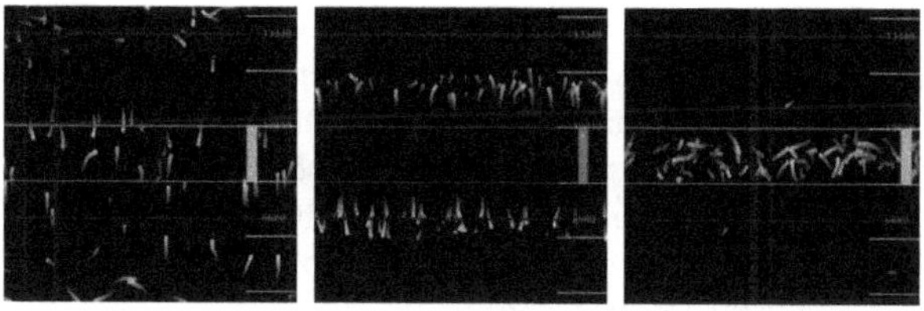

(a) Magnetic mode. (b) Repel mode. (c) Drag mode.

**Figure 2.7:** Modes can be assigned to frequency bands.

is, in fact, a very typical example for the unique sonic possibilities that arise from the TouchNoise approach.

The *repel* mode is the opposite of the magnetic mode. Particles within the effect range are expelled from touches. This effect induces holes in the stereophonic frequency spectrum.

Not only do the different interaction modes produce sound effects while they are active on the playground, but also on their release, as this releases the particles back to their default behavior. Each of these functionalities can further be assigned to whole frequency bands, as shown in figure 2.7. A further function that is applicable exclusively to frequency bands is the *quantization*. In this mode, particles that pass the band play only the center frequency of the band instead of a continuous glissando. This leads to an accentuation of frequencies and reduces the level of micro tonality. The activation time of frequency bands can be limited. The division of the frequency bands can be adjusted to different (musical) scales. This includes a linear division into up to 40 equally sized bands, a pentatonic, a pythagorean and a chromatic scale.

The combination of TouchNoise's functions enables complex sonic behaviors. Some interactions exclude others and/or require a precise execution without any distraction or side effects. Those are the creation and deletion of particles and flow fields. The modes *accentuate*, *drag*, *magnetic*, *repel*, and *quantization*, however, can be combined with each other, for touches as well as for frequency bands. Only the combination of *drag* and *repel* and of *quantization* and *repel* are excluded for frequency bands as both, *drag* and *quantization*, affect particles that are within a frequency band which is empty due to the repellant force.

Multiple modes and motion rules might conflict with each other. The user might, for instance, want to drag particles that follow a flow field and are at the same time attracted by a frequency band. In order to cope with such situations in a reasonable way, we decided to prioritize all influences according to the directness of their assignment. Touch interactions are of paramount importance, hence highest priority, and dominate all other influences. Frequency band functionality is located on the second level of the hierarchy. The rules of the particle motion (Brownian motion, flow field and flocking mechanisms) described in section 2.3.2 have the lowest priority.

TouchNoise further implements a MIDI connection. Currently, three modes are implemented that process MIDI messages in different ways. The *Key mode* and *Frequency mode* provide another way of assigning certain functionalities (magnetic, repel, drag, accentuation, and quantization) to frequency bands. In *Key mode*, the keys of the MIDI keyboard are mapped index-wise to the frequency bands. In *Frequency mode*, the pitch value is taken to select the frequency band that contains this pitch. As long as a key on a MIDI keyboard is pressed, certain functions are assigned to the corresponding frequency band—key release deassigns the function. In the *Add mode*, particles are created at the precise pitch position, which then behave as all particles but are deleted subsequent to the key release.

### 2.3.4 The User Interface

The various functions of TouchNoise are accessed through the graphical user interface shown in figure 2.8. It consists of the playground, a particle menu, different *effect range and toggle widgets*, a motion menu, a piano bar, and various buttons and sliders. All interface widgets are arranged with regard to their priority, i.e. how often they are used when playing with TouchNoise. Those functions that are frequently needed where placed at the lower edge of the screen. Rarely needed functions are on the upper edge. The particle playground in the center of the interface is the essential part of TouchNoise. It displays the particles and enables direct interaction with them. The playground's lower and upper borders correspond to the lowest and highest frequency that the particles can reach, and are specified by two moveable handles.

Settings that are related to the particles are accessed via an extendable circular particle menu, which is shown in figure 2.9. This includes the particle lifetime (no. 4 in figure 2.9), the maximal Brownian angle (no. 5 in 2.9), the particle speed (no. 6 in figure 2.9), the number of particles (no. 2 and 7 in figure 2.9, adjusting this slider creates and deletes particles at random positions), and the activation

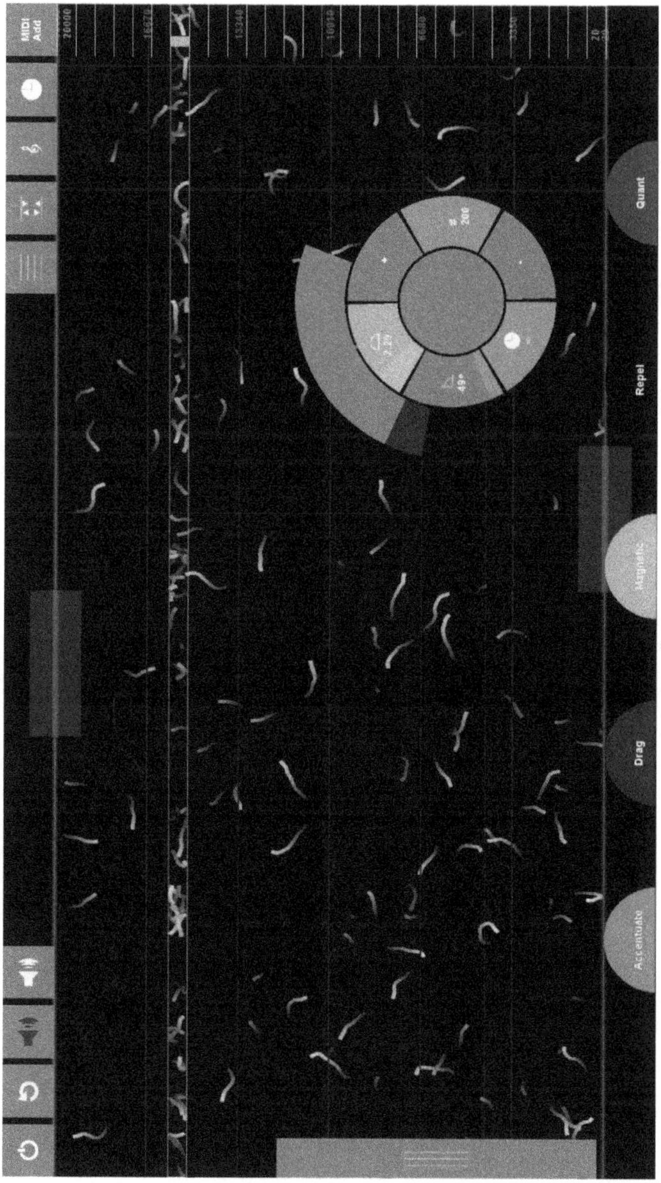


**Figure 2.8:** A screenshot of TouchNoise's graphical user interface. A frequency band has an active drag function. Accentuation and magnetic mode are active for direct touch interaction within the particle playground. The circular particle menu is also open; it can be freely dragged over the screen and minimizes when put at or flicked to the border.

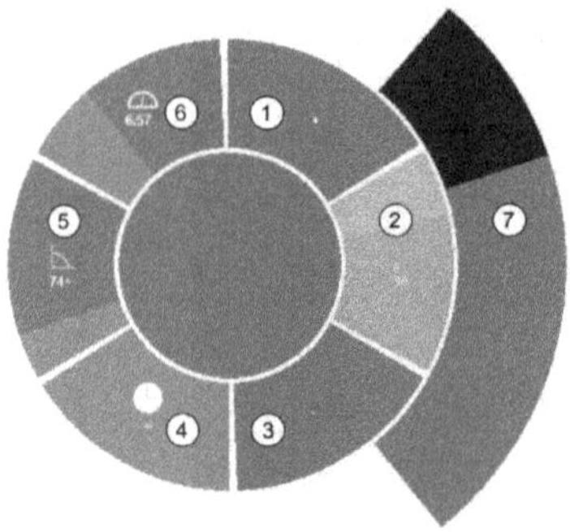


Figure 2.9: The particle menu is implemented as a two-stage circular menu.

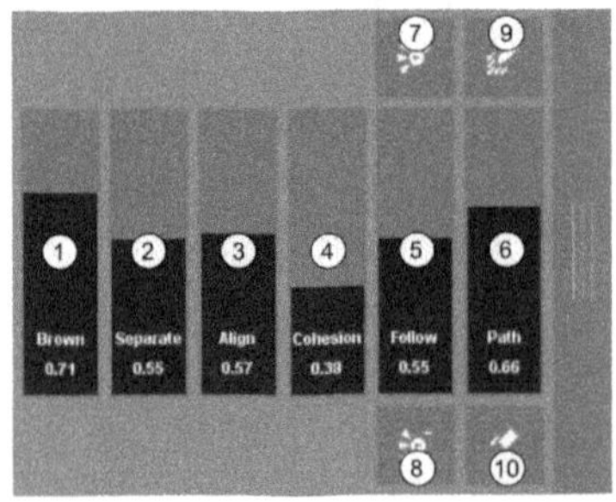


**Figure 2.10:** The motion menu is implemented as a *flip back panel.*

of the modes for adding or removing particles to and from the playground at touch positions on the playground (no. 1 and 3 in figure 2.9).

In its initial, inactive state the particle menu is minimized, only its inner circle is shown. The menu switches automatically into this state when it is dragged at or flicked towards a screen edge. When dragged back into the screen, it switches into extended state, as displayed in figure 2.9. The menu makes up a two-stage circular menu. The first-level control elements are only buttons that activate either a certain mode (no. 1 and 3 in 2.9) or a circular bent slider for value selection on the second level (no. 7 in figure 2.9). Once a slider is visible, the user can change its value by tap or drag gestures. Especially the Brownian angle is well represented as a 360° slider. Slider activation (tapping the button) and slider adjustment (tap or drag at the slider) can also be performed as one continuous drag gesture starting at the button. Thereby, we facilitate a more fluent interaction that lets the user rapidly return to the work on the playground. The inner circle of the particle menu serves as a handle to manipulation of the menu itself. By performing a drag gesture on the inner circle, the particle menu can be shifted over the screen. In this way, the distance between the control elements and the interaction space can be kept at a minimum, and undesired occlusions are easy to fix. A pinch gesture on the inner circle scales the menu. This can increase and decrease its size and playground occlusion.

Another novel interface widget implemented in TouchNoise is the *flip back panel* (see figure 2.10). In its hidden state, only its handle is visible, as shown at the left margin of figure 2.8. The sliders in this panel indicate the weightings of the

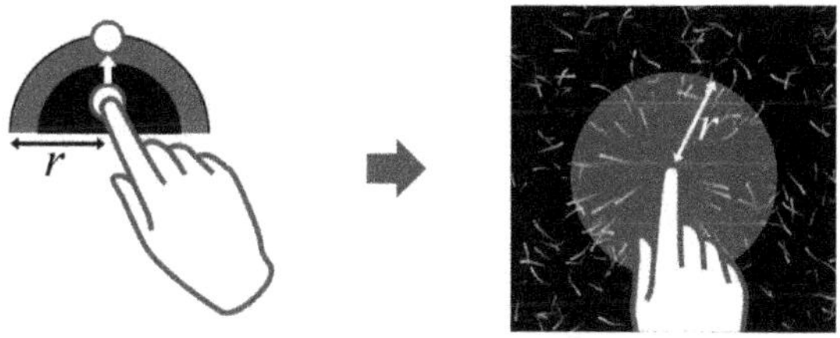


**Figure 2.11:** Manipulation of the effect range of touch interactions on the playground via the *effect range and toggle widget*.

different particle motion rules. Their settings are typically done once in a while, and then interaction returns to the playground. Following this, we decided to eliminate the necessity of closing the panel, i.e. dragging it back off the screen. Instead, the user opens it with the drag gesture that is typical for panels and holds it with one hand, while operating the sliders with the other hand. When released, it flips back automatically, like an elastic band. The layout of the linear sliders is conceived, so that several sliders can be manipulated at once with multiple fingers of one hand. The menu includes sliders to set the weightings of the motion principles (no. 1-6 in figure 2.10), and buttons to activate the corresponding modes for adding and removing leader particles and for drawing and erasing vector fields (no. 7-10 in figure 2.10).

With the *effect range and toggle widgets* (on the bottom margin of figure 2.8) we introduce a new interface widget that provides three functions. Basically, it behaves like a toggle button that is triggered by tapping. Thereby, the direct interaction modes (accentuation, drag, magnetic, repel, and quantization) are (de-)activated for touch interaction on the playground. Secondly, the modes can be assigned to frequency bands by the bimanual gestures shown in figure 2.12. Thirdly, these widgets are used to set the range of the corresponding effects by a drag gesture starting on the button area, and then moving out of it (see figure 2.11). A transparent circular field indicates the effect range, that the interaction will have on the playground at a ratio of 1:1. Releasing the touch sets the radius and the transparent field disappears.

The *piano bar* at the right margin of the playground displays the division of the frequency domain into discrete frequency bands (in figure 2.8 there are 29 bands). Activation of a band is done through a bimanual gesture (see figure 2.12), by tapping and holding the effect range and toggle widget, and tapping or dragging over the piano bar to assign the effect to one or more bands. To activate

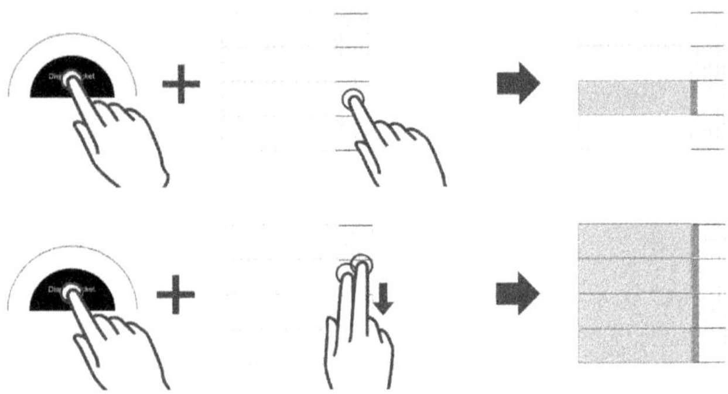

**Figure 2.12:** Bimanual gestures to assign effects to frequency bands.

them all, a two-finger drag downward, or upward for complete deactivation is performed. This is especially useful for a fine-grained piano bar. Here, the Fat Finger Problem occurs. The piano bar requires precisely performed gestures. Therefore it should be operated by the dominant hand that has finer motor skills, which is the right hand for most users (Raymond, Pontier, Dufour & Moller 1996). Hence, the piano bar is placed at the right side of the playground and typically controlled by right hand.

The MIDI button (top right in figure 2.8) enables the use of MIDI controllers. This allows a different approach to TouchNoise. The controllers give the user a more haptic feeling. They enable the user to connect familiar structures such as the layout of keys on a piano with TouchNoise. The MIDI button reacts to touches like a regular button, but has some additional functionalities. Different effect modes are assigned to the button in the same way as they are assigned to frequency bands (figure 2.12), with a tap and hold gesture on an effect widget and a tap on the MIDI button. The changing of the current MIDI mode is done by a tap on the button.

The remaining interface elements are positioned above the playground. They offer different functionalities that are likely to be performed less frequently. The button on the top left corner of the screen closes the application. Next to it, the reset button is placed, which reverts all playground settings to their initial state. It is followed by the two buttons that open the sliders for the manipulation of basic volume level and accentuation level. The next button alters the mapping between playground and frequency domain between linear and logarithmic, whereas its neighboring button enables the mode to distort this mapping manually by pinch gestures. Frequency bands are organized with the two following buttons. The first of them gives access to different (musical) scales (linear, pentatonic, pythagorean, and chromatic), and the second button activates a slider to adjust the activation time of the frequency bands.

### 2.3.5 Playing TouchNoise

TouchNoise's sound output derives from the particle system. Every particle creates a sine signal. All signals are added and produce the sound of TouchNoise. The distribution of the particles on the playground and the particle system's dynamics define the stereophonic frequency spectrum that is output. When the particles are equally distributed, white noise-like output is generated. When there are only few particles active on the playground, the single sine signals become distinguishable instead of a diffuse noise spectrum. The number of particles and their (initial) distribution can be influenced by the user. Particles can be added and deleted by touch gestures directly on the playground and, thus, they can be placed at explicit positions which allows the definition of an initial distribution and noise shape, respectively.

Another influencing factor on the number of particles is their lifetime. A short lifetime allows the user to create short sonic clusters at only a few frequencies, just like seeding sonic energy. The further behavior of this nest can be determined by advanced motion settings, which control the agility of the particles and the way they spread out over the playground. A vector field defines the direction, flocking keeps the cluster together, Brownian angle and particle speed affect the volatility.

The clustering of particles puts emphasis on certain frequencies and on specific positions in the stereo sound field. Particle accumulations can be induced by flocking, magnetic and drag interaction, and by limiting the area of particle motion. Repellent interaction and accentuations with an accentuation level set to 0 create holes in the spectrum, which also emphasizes the remaining frequencies. The particle system reacts with a continuous behavior to each touch and frequency band interaction. The motion settings specify the pace of reactions. Just as the typical behavior of any instrument, this makes up TouchNoise's peculiarities with which the user can play creatively. TouchNoise's strengths lie in the interplay of the different behavioral possibilities of the particle system and the various interactions. We can only pinpoint some of these productive combinations here to give an impression of the range of possibilities.

Even though the basic sound is noise, TouchNoise can also create tonal spectra. In quantization mode, the frequency domain is discretized to only those frequencies that derive from certain scales. Not all frequency bands have to be set to quantization mode, mixtures of quantized and "glissando" bands are possible, too. The different musical scales reduce the micro tonality of TouchNoise and create various harmonicities and tonalities. Again, the combination with limited particle lifetime and flocking creates musically interesting, very harmonic and even melodious effects.

A very useful combination of direct interaction modes is the drag and magnetic mode combination. Thereby particles are collected by attractive forces and can then be dragged over the playground. The extreme accumulation and the different speed compared to the unaffected particles make the affected particles and the gestures they perform clearly audible. The adjustment of the radii while exerting an effect leads to interesting sonic structures. As an example, adjusting the repel radius leads to new transition sounds, while retreating or coming closer again.

Playing with the priorities of the interactions, that influence the particle motion, is another approach of creating interesting sound effects. Dragging particles out of a magnetic frequency band, and releasing them, leads to the particles heading directly back to the frequency band, i.e. straight glissandi. The particle speed specifies how fast these glissandi are performed. When the same frequency band is also accentuated with a zero accentuation level, the particles disappear at the moment they enter the band.

Interesting sound effects are not only caused by the exertion of the different functions, but also by their termination. Releasing a magnetic touch causes the very narrow sound cluster—which often has a whistling sound—to expand and gradually fade back into an increasingly broad, noisy spectrum. Even though this is conceptually similar to opening a bandpass filter on a noise signal, the momentum of the particle system and the precise sine signals lead to a very unique sound, that cannot be replicated with filters.

Some functions can be used to pass particles to other functions, e.g. dragging, attracting or adding particles to the starting point of a flow path. Particles can also be added to the path by using the MIDI Add mode to create sweep sounds.

Musically very interesting, especially for creating pad sounds, is the assignment of the magnetic function to the MIDI keys. Now "magnetic chords" can be played into a noise spectrum. The noise fades into the tonal sound played, and when the keys are released, back into noise. Again this invites to experiment with the dynamics of the particle system, adjusting the particle speed and Brownian angle to specify the pace of the sound transitions. Let us now assume that these "magnetic chords" are played into an empty playground, and that the particle lifetime is limited to only one second. Particles may now be created via tap and drag gestures on and around the frequency bands or chord notes, respectively. This creates very lively and harmonic sounds that evolve over the stereo panorama, and is enriched by little glide sounds around the precise pitches, whenever a particle is created apart from these.

## 2.4 Discussion

In our early experiences with TouchNoise we focussed on the possibilities of noise modulation with a particle system. Since we wanted to facilitate a direct and easy interaction with the particles, TouchNoise was designed for multitouch screens right from the beginning. However, the first graphical user interface consisted of various control elements that mainly adapted the behavior of traditional WIMP elements[5], and did not exploit the potential of a real multitouch interface. Most functionality was hidden in overloaded panels that occluded a large part of the playground. Effect radius settings on a slider-like interface element suffered from a scale conflict, when the widget indicated a downscaled instead of the actual effect range. The early version of the piano bar was a sprawling, fiddly matrix of buttons.

Therefore, TouchNoise went through an extensive revision process which has been detailed by Berndt et al. (2015). Our aim was to ease TouchNoise's functionality and to create a more direct access, fostering direct interaction with the particle system on the playground. The direct manipulation via touch gestures is a natural form of interaction, that we know from the physical world. Quite often the term "natural user interface" is used in this context. However, some of the newly created control elements and the required bimanual gestures may not be obvious to novice users, and need introduction, e.g. through a printed tutorial or demonstration video.

The graphical user interface of TouchNoise is oriented towards a user standing on the bottom edge of the screen. According to Fitts' Law (Fitts 1954), a target, here it is an interface widget, is easier to reach the closer it is to the user and the bigger the target's size is. Therefore, often used control elements are

[5]WIMP stands for an interface paradigm that builds upon the elements windows, icons, menus, and pointers/pointing devices.

placed at the lower edge and less frequently needed elements are placed at the upper edge of the screen. Even though the graphical user interface of TouchNoise is developed to scale to many screen resolutions, there is a restriction that must be made. Deriving from the Fat Finger Problem, we recommend a screen width of at least 18.3 centimeters and a height of at least 16.7 centimeters. This guarantees that all interface elements have a size that covers the contact area of a fingertip on the screen, which is 1 centimeter on average (Saffer 2008). We tested TouchNoise on 13, 27, and 32 inch screens and also briefly on a wall-sized display. Especially the 32 inch screen turned to feature a convenient size. On the one hand, the display is big enough for differentiated, sweeping gestures and it allows precise interactions. This makes this size most suitable for live performances. On the other hand, it is small enough for the user to reach every spot on the screen without much effort.

For presentation, TouchNoise can be displayed on a second screen or via onstage projection. The combination of gestural interaction, auditory and visual presentation makes TouchNoise a very performative interface. It mediates a feeling of mastery and is, thus, attractive for audiences, too. Due to its orientation, the instrument is most appropriate for a single performer. There are further possible developments, which support collaborative use of TouchNoise. Creating different layers of playgrounds that can be shifted over the screen is one option. In a multi-user scenario large multitouch display walls can be a further option, as here the interface's orientation is equal to all users.

MIDI controllers offer many possibilities to interact with TouchNoise. They complement the multitouch interface with concepts, such as the piano keyboard, that are well-known to musicians. Such controllers provide more differentiating tactile feedback than a multitouch screen. TouchNoise's usability might further be increased by complex gestures (e.g. blob detection can enrich the library of gestures) and additional input modalities. Marker-tracked tangibles on the display can be used as alternatives to touches, as used by the Reactable interface (Kaltenbranner, Jorda, Geiger & Alonso 2006, Geiger, Alber, Jordà & Alonso 2010), the ReacTacT system (Ó Nuanáin & O'Sullivan 2014) and others.

With the revision of TouchNoise we increased the user's influence on the particle behavior. In the first version of TouchNoise only Brownian motion was implemented. Here, the interaction affected the particle system always immediately and the effect stopped immediately after releasing the touches. Due to the newly added functions, longterm behaviors can be defined, e.g. with the help of vector fields.

Due to the possibility of combining the different functions and their priorities, a lot of configurations with different sonic effects exist. On the one hand, this might overwhelm the user, but on the other hand, it gives freedom to experiment and provides the open-endedness that is of key importance for longterm engagement. The addition of a simplified TouchNoise setup or different preset configurations could help novice users to become acquainted with the instrument.

A technical challenge of TouchNoise is its resource-demanding sound synthesis. Each particle is technically represented by an oscillator, a stereo panner and envelope generators for continuous amplitude and frequency transitions. Together with the various functionalities for motion and interaction, the number of particles must be limited to ensure proper output without glitches. Our development system (Intel Core i7-3770 CPU (3.40GHz), 16GB RAM, GeForce GTX 680, standard sound chip, 3M multitouch screen) allows a maximum of 200 particles.

The multitude of functionalities causes a lot of options to expand TouchNoise. This includes the opportunity to further customize given modes (e.g. setting the yet constant neighborhood distance for the swarming behaviors). Combining existing functions might be another possibility to upgrade TouchNoise. The assignment of interaction functions such as magnetic or repel to single particles, swarms or paths could allow interesting new behaviors.

Further developments should intensify the focus on the horizontal axis of the playground, i.e. the work with effects in the stereo sound field. The piano bar can also be interesting as a horizontal interface element and in combination with the vertical piano bar. It is, yet, unclear whether the stereo panning is the best parameter of sound synthesis that could be mapped to the horizontal axis.

Due to the stochastic aspects of TouchNoise's behavior it is not trivial, if not impossible, to reproduce certain effects in exactly the same way. This may be typical for such an active musical instrument, but it complicates the composing of (reproducible) music for it. Setting a configuration and performing the same interactions might be as difficult as writing them down in detail. A possible approach might be to film the whole performance. This requires an external camera, because gestures are difficult to recognize without seeing the player's hands. Another possibility is to write down the instructions. As some interactions need eye contact for precise performance, especially if they desire adaptation to the stochastic behavior of the particle system, it is difficult to reproduce a musical piece while receiving the video or written instructions. A more suitable notation system might evolve with further experiences.

## 2.5 Summary

With modern technology a new generation of digital musical instruments evolved. Their sound is not directly generated by a physical process, as in case of traditional musical instruments, but it is generated by algorithms. Multitouch screens are one possibility to visualize these algorithms and control them. Various musical applications for mobile devices exist, many of them feature a certain autonomy in their functionality. The degree of interactivity of these instruments varies. Often, a particle system is a key element of these applications. Sometimes, these particle systems are based on flocking behavior.

TouchNoise is a fully-fledged multitouch-driven digital musical instrument. It offers a new interface for noise modulation through the interaction with a particle system. Each particle represents an oscillator that generates a sine signal according to the particle's position on the playground. Its frequency derives from the vertical position, and its position in the stereo sound field from the horizontal position. The sum of all sine signals produces TouchNoise's sound output. The particles feature autonomous behavior according to several principles, including Brownian motion, flocking behavior (align, separate, follow, cohesion) and a flow field. Besides the character of motion, the sound depends on various factors, such as the number and distribution of particles or the frequency mapping (linear, logarithmic, quantized, etc.).

The user can interact directly with the particles by dragging, attracting, repelling, or accentuating them. These functions can also be assigned to frequency bands. Interactions with frequency bands are basically complex operations, but in TouchNoise they are directly accessible and easily executable by bimanual gestures. Several new interface widgets were developed (effect range and toggle widget, the piano bar, flip back panel). The graphical user interface has been designed under consideration of the high priority of each interface element. This layout pays off with faster, more direct, and fluent interaction. The extension of TouchNoise with MIDI controllers represents an additional input modality, which introduces familiar musical concepts to the TouchNoise interface.

During a yearlong series of practical test and demo sessions with TouchNoise, we gained many inspirations for future directions and further development. The aim now is to gain more detailed experience through the cooperation with composers and musicians, who acquire practical and artistic experiences with TouchNoise.

**Acknowledgement** The authors like to thank Raimund Dachselt, head of the Interactive Media Lab Dresden at Technische Universität Dresden. His constructive feedback, creative discussions and ideas were a valuable input during TouchNoise's interface conception.

## Bibliography

Ó Nuanáin, C. & O'Sullivan, L. (2014), Real-time Algorithmic Composition with a Tabletop Musical Interface—A First Prototype and Performance, *in* 'Audio Mostly 2014: 9th Conf. on Interaction with Sound—Imagining Sound and Music', Aalborg University, Interactive Institute/Sonic Studio Piteå, ACM, Aalborg, Denmark.

Al-Kassab, N. (2013), Multitouch-Interaktion mit Klangpartikeln, student research project, Technische Universität Dresden, Faculty of Computer Science, Dresden, Germany.

Al-Kassab, N. (2014), Ein Multitouch-Interface für ein digitales Musikinstrument, Diploma thesis, Technische Universität Dresden, Faculty of Computer Science, Dresden, Germany.

Berndt, A., Al-Kassab, N. & Dachselt, R. (2014), TouchNoise: A Particle-based Multitouch Noise Modulation Interface, *in* 'Proc. of New Interfaces for Musical Expression (NIME) 2014', Goldsmiths, University of London, London, UK, pp. 323–326.

Berndt, A., Al-Kassab, N. & Dachselt, R. (2015), TouchNoise: A New Multitouch Interface for Creative Work with Noise, *in* 'Audio Mostly 2015: 10th Conf. on Interaction with Sound—Sound, Semantics and Social Interaction', Aristotle University of Tessaloniki, ACM, Tessaloniki, Greece.

Bisig, D., Schacher, J. C. & Neukom, M. (2011), Flowspace – A Hybrid Ecosystem, *in* 'Proc. of New Interfaces for Musical Expression (NIME) 2011', University of Oslo, Norwegian Academy of Music, Oslo, Norway, pp. 260–263.

Blackwell, T. M. & Young, M. W. (2004), 'Self-Organised Music', *Organized Sound* **9**(2), 123–136.

Choi, H. & Wang, G. (2010), LUSH: An Organic Eco + Music System, *in* 'Proc. of New Interfaces for Musical Expression (NIME) 2010', University of Technology Sydney, Sydney, Australia, pp. 112–115.

Dika, N. (2014), 'Photophore Synth', Taika Systems Ltd. app on iTunes, v1.0.

Eno, B. & Chilvers, P. (2011*a*), 'Bloom', Opal Limited. app on iTunes, v2.1.1.

Eno, B. & Chilvers, P. (2011*b*), 'Trope', Opal Limited. app on iTunes, v1.2.

Eno, B. & Chilvers, P. (2014), 'Scape', Opal Limited. app on iTunes, v1.1.

Fitts, P. M. (1954), 'The Information Capacity of the Human Motor System in Controlling the Amplitude of Movement', *Journal of Experimental Psychology* **47**(6), 381–391.

Geiger, G., Alber, N., Jordà, S. & Alonso, M. (2010), 'The Reactable: A Collaborative Musical Instrument for Playing and Understanding Music', *Her&Mus. Heritage & Museography* pp. 36–43.

Kaltenbranner, M., Jorda, S., Geiger, G. & Alonso, M. (2006), The reacTable*: A Collaborative Musical Instrument, *in* '15th IEEE Int. Workshops on Enabling Technologies: Infrastructure for Collaborative Enterprises (WETICE'06)', pp. 406–411.

Kuhara, Y. & Kobayashi, D. (2011), Kinetic Particles Synthesizer Using Multi-Touch Screen Interface of Mobile Devices, *in* 'Proc. of New Interfaces for Musical Expression (NIME) 2011', University of Oslo, Norwegian Academy of Music, Oslo, Norway, pp. 136–137.

Nash, A. (2013), 'Love like rain'. last accessed: June 2015.
**URL:** *http://yamanakanash.net/*

O'Neill, S. & Chilvers, P. (2012), 'Air', Opal Limited. app on iTunes, v1.3.

Raymond, M., Pontier, D., Dufour, A.-B. & Moller, A. P. (1996), 'Frequency-Dependent Maintenance of Left Handedness in Humans', *The Royal Society Proceedings: Biological Sciences* **263**(1377), 1627–1633.

Reynolds, C. W. (1987), 'Flocks, Herds and Schools: A Distributed Behavioral Model', *ACM SIGGRAPH Computer Graphics* **21**(4), 25–34.

Reynolds, C. W. (2007), 'Boids: Background and Update'. last accessed: June 2015.
**URL:** *http://www.red3d.com/cwr/boids/*

Rosenbaum, E. (2011), MelodyMorph: A Reconfigurable Musical Instrument, *in* 'Proc. of New Interfaces for Musical Expression (NIME) 2011', University of Oslo, Norwegian Academy of Music, Oslo, Norway, pp. 445–447.

Saffer, D. (2008), *Designing Gestural Interfaces: Touchscreens and Interactive Devices*, O'Reilly, Sebastopol, CA.

Sandler, S. & Windl, J. (2013), 'NodeBeat', app for iOS, Blackberry, Android, and Windows.

Taylor, C. (2012), 'GenMu Box', Carl Taylor Mobile Development. app on iTunes.

Maxim Müller

Chapter 3

# Interactive Ambient Music Generation

**Abstract** When it comes to composition and performance, conventional music is limited to the physical presence of competent musicians and their instruments. If nothing else, this kind of music is unique, not easy to reproduce and restricted in time and storability; not to mention interactivity. This work introduces a concept for Ambient music creation. An insight into the history of the Ambient genre and the analysis of representative songs reveal their specific properties. With the help of four music generation paradigms, those findings lead to a song synthesizer consisting of five song elements, each playing a specific role in the polyphonic composition. To provide an interactively changeable composition algorithm and a great variety of expressive characters as many controllable musical parameters have been built in. The music generated in this way is potentially infinite and non-repetitive. The concept not only allows for an experimental exploration of the expressive potentials of the composition algorithm, but also provides the storage of expression related parameter sets. Thus it is able to adapt to interactive contexts, e.g. video games.

## 3.1 Introduction

Music is more than the sum of its parts, it develops in different ways and always depends on the listener's mind. That is because our brains are not only capable of evaluating sound objectively in its acoustic nature, but also to interpret it in an emotional way. This interpretation is highly subjective because it depends on the context of the music's appearance and the listener's experience. However, some musical properties are linked to physical aspects of the human body, e.g. rhythm of heartbeats and breath. This allows a universal consensus (Kungel 2008) and makes music one of the most beautiful forms of emotional communication. This particular ability of music has its price: it is time consuming; not only the listening (a) or the effort to understand, also—and especially—the creation (b). Two essential requirements for the creation of music are an adequate amount of musical education and physical presence. Despite all this effort, music is—once composed—finite, unique and without expert knowledge not appropriately controllable or editable (Berndt 2011): a disadvantage even digital storage technologies could not leave behind. These problems were first addressed by algorithmic music generation also called generative music (b). The desire to provide a listener with high-quality music that does not stress his attention (a) led to the birth of a new genre called Ambient music.

The aim of this work is to create a concept for flexible algorithmic Ambient music creation. It is based on previous work of Müller (2013) and Berndt (2014). The algorithm itself should not only be changeable in its emotional character of expression, but also realtime interactive in as many musical features as possible. That is what differentiates this concept from related work.

The first aim of this chapter is to provide a deeper understanding of the yet rather unexplored typicalities of Ambient. Therefore, several Ambient pieces have been studied and rules for their generation identified. In the following showcase pieces of Brian Eno will be analyzed in detail. In section 3.3 an introductory overview of music generation approaches will be given and discussed in the context of interactive Ambient generation. Further related works are presented in section 3.4. Our approach to this is then detailed and discussed in the remainder of this chapter.

## 3.2 Characteristics of Ambient

This section analyses exemplary Ambient pieces in order to determine necessary clues for the generation of ambient music.

Between 1978 and 1982 Brian Eno, former member of the band Roxy Music and an exponent of John Cage's philosophy of Noise music, created his albums Ambient 1–4. These provide a genre-defining musical abstract of the whole genre. With Ambient Eno gave a revival to Eric Satie's *musique d'ameublement*/furniture music (Schulze 2000, Collins & d'Escriván 2007) who wanted music to not only get integrated in the daily routine, but also to provide a fixed function like a bed or a chair depending on its spatial context.

> "My intention is to produce original pieces ostensibly (but not exclusively) for particular times and situations with a view to building up a small but versatile catalogue of environmental music suited to a wide variety of moods and atmospheres."[1]

In the 1970s it was hard to win record labels for this new kind of music with its lack of beat, melody, and vocals (Holmes 2012). Nowadays, its great diversity makes Ambient a widely accepted genre, combining influences from Jazz, Electronica, House and others. There is a great variety of ambient sub genres, e.g. the heavenly Space Music, noisy Illbient, the industrial-like Dark Ambient, Live-Ambient, Ambient Dub, only to name a few. According to Holmes, they all share a common element:

> "If there is a unifying element in all ambient music it appears to be a continuity of energy that enables a suspension of tension. Like minimalism, contemporary ambient music often relies on a persistent rhythm and slowly evolving wash of sound textures."[2]

Frequently observed musical characteristics of Ambient are listed in the following without any claim to comprehensiveness. This is based on analyses of albums of genre representatives including "Ambient 1: Music for Airports", "Ambient 2: The Plateaux of Mirror", "Ambient 4: On Land"[3] and "Lux" by Brian Eno, the "Ambient Soundscapes and Rhythmic Journeys"[4] by Thom Brennan as well as video game soundtracks for "Riven" (Miller 1998) and "The Elder Scrolls V: Skyrim" (Soule 2011). A more detailed version of this analysis is given by Berndt (2014).

The used sound properties are a first remarkable characteristic which can be found in almost all Ambient music pieces. There are three major classes: bell-like amplitude envelopes, slow pad sounds and natural sounds. The bell-like sounds are classified by very short attack and long continuous release phases that appear to be endless. Typical examples are pianos, bells, vibraphones, and harps. The dominant sounds in Ambient 1 are piano and bell. Figure 3.1 shows the frequency spectrogram of the first seconds of track "1/1" which reflect the properties of the whole piece. Despite the unpredictability of the sounds and the missing measure, piano and bells are synchronized with a few minor exceptions

[1] Brian Eno cited by Milkowski (1983), page 16.
[2] Holmes (2012), page 377.
[3] Further referred to as Ambient 1, Ambient 2 and Ambient 4.
[4] `http://www.thombrennan.com/`, last accessed: June 2015.

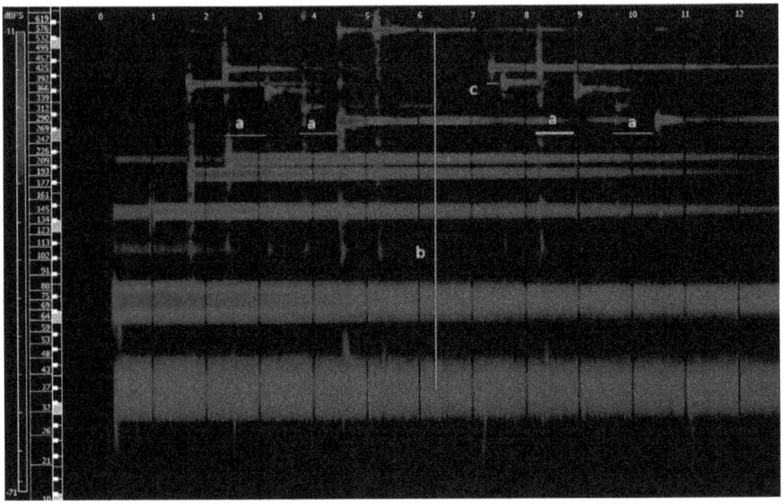


**Figure 3.1:** Extract of the frequency spectrogram of Ambient 1 track "1/1". (a) Inter-onset intervals. (b) Pitch range from D0 to D4. (c) Sole exception from the rhythm.

(figure 3.1(c)). The short attack phases can easily be identified from the clear left ends of energy bursts in the frequency bands. One can also see the continuous, never audibly ending release phases and the whole-piece-wrapping reverberation by the long stretched, soft blurring to the right of the bursts. Extraordinarily memorable is the figure that recurs in the same position over and over again, a motif. In the Ambient genre recurrent structures have a long periodicity and vary each time.

Another typical type of sounds are the soft in and out fading sound layers like pad sounds, string layers, synthetic layers or choirs. Modulations of amplitude, frequency and filters are often used to make the otherwise rigid pad sounds more vivid. These sounds are mostly played in chords or have a chord-like tonal structure. Ambient 1 track "2/1", for instance, consists of only choir sounds, single tones which all repeat with a fixed period. Figure 3.2 depicts the spectrum of the first minute. One can see the constant periodicity of the single tones as well as their soft attack and release from the blurry ends of the lines. The spectra of the repeated tones are identical, so the tones must have been recorded once and then looped. All in all the song contains seven different tones.

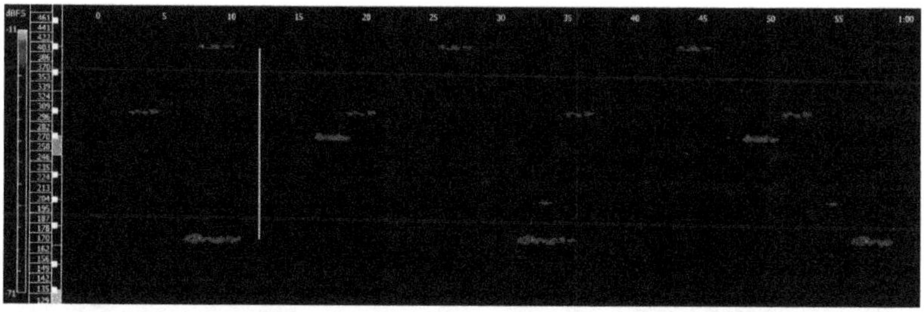

**Figure 3.2:** Extract of the frequency spectrum of Ambient 1 track "2/1". Harmonics have been omitted to avoid irritations. The green markings indicate the pitch range from F2 to G#3.

Nature sounds that appear in several Ambient pieces, are not dominating the genre, though. They do not appear in the majority of the analyzed pieces. Ambient 4, however, combines modulated electronic sounds and nature sounds. "The Elder Scrolls V" does the same; it combines both music and nature sounds. Besides periodical phenomena like the breaking of sea waves, natural sounds normally do not follow rhythmical patterns and are not synchronized with the music. Figure 3.3 shows an extract of the spectrum in the middle of Ambient 4 track "Unfamiliar Wind (Leeks Hills)". A damped sine modulating the bass tone is clearly visible in figure 3.3(b). Even the synthetic sounds are slightly modulated (figure 3.3(d)). The tones have similar attack and release phases that overlap and create indistinguishable flowing sounds. A human voice plays sporadically. Randomly occurring sounds of human mumble and varying animal sounds constantly accompany the main instrument. Thom Brennan's music features some further instances of synthetic effect sounds.

Monophonic sounds, however, are quite rare. More popular are sounds with few harmonics, that are less bright and less intrusive as observed on the album Lux with its bass-heavy piano sounds. Another ambient characteristic is the frequent use of reverberation in order to create an impression of spatial wideness and timelessness, which is also supported by the frequent and comparably long rests. They last up to ten seconds and may contain silence but more often fading out tones. These rests also make it hard to recognize and follow melodic structures.

Recurrent structures with short attacks often occur as arpeggiated chords. They create continuously sounding, rhythmic sound textures, which are subtly varied by, for instance, random permutation as observed in the case of Ambient 2 track

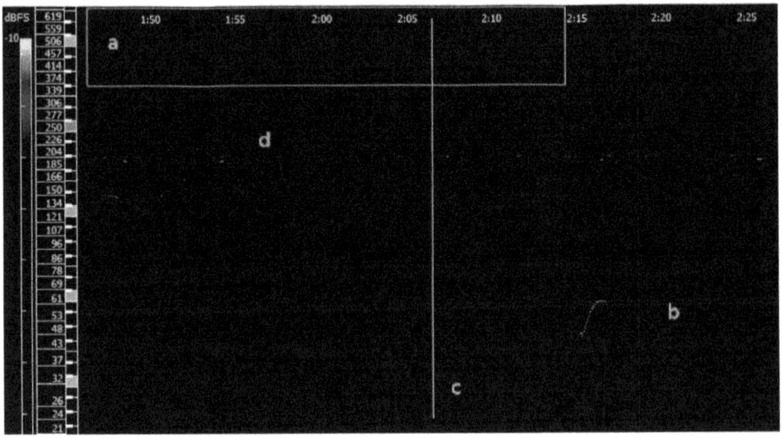


**Figure 3.3:** Extract of the frequency spectrum of Ambient 4 track "Unfamiliar Wind (Leeks Hills)". (a) Human voice. (b) Frequency-modulated bass. (c) Pitch ranges from A1 to D#4. (d) Synthesizer soundscape with effect sounds.

"First Light". But there are also non-melodic tone sequences that may spread over several octaves, without revealing a horizontal structure. This expresses the equality of all sound events. A tonal center is not to be determined, neither are remarkable dramatical target points, which the music may usually lead to, thus the listener should not be able to orient himself. Yet these tone sequences are the result of well-defined algorithmic processes like parallel sound loops (as in Ambient 1 "2/1") of different lengths or fractal processes (as in Ambient 2 "First Light").

The harmonic structure is mostly minimalistic. The pieces are often dominated only by one chord that feeds all instruments enabling long fading, multi-overlapping sound layers that still fit together harmonically. Ambient music tends to stagger around a harmonic state, neither reaching nor leaving it. It creates a mood and keeps it alive. The musical structure resembles a slow breathing with phases of condensed sound events and phases of relieve that celebrate the fading of sounds. A deeper hierarchy or complex nesting cannot be found, though.

Even on a time scale the purpose of infinity and detachedness can be identified. Many ambient pieces do not have a regular meter. Sound events seem to occur randomly and non-rhythmically. Therefore, a classical tempo analysis is futile. It cannot reflect the often subjectively perceived slow tempo. Long fade-ins make it impossible to propagate a precise onset detection and measure.

In his analysis of Brian Eno's works Eric Tamm (1995) summarizes the stylistic properties of Ambient music with this concise, accurate description:

> "Certain traits characterize most pieces composed in the ambient style: quietness, gentleness, an emphasis on the vertical color of sound, establishment and maintenance of a single pervasive atmosphere, non-developmental forms, regularly or irregularly repeating events or cycles of events, modal pitch-sets, choice of a few limited parameters for each piece, layered textures tending towards an even balance of tone and noise, and a pulse that is sometimes uneven, sometimes 'breathing', and sometimes non-existent."[5]

All analyzed pieces share a peculiar commonality: several mostly repetitive sound patterns within local musical structures (mostly chords) that coexist but are rhythmically independent. In many cases the only connection is the tonal material that derives from the underlying chord such that no "dissonances" occur. These elements are synchronized, especially the sounds with short attack phases. Those sounds with long attack and release phases may start independently because they catch no attention. Due to the frequent repetition of the elements, the song structures are barely established and the length of a piece seems arbitrary.

The listener does not need a contextual knowledge covering more than a few seconds before or after the current playback position thanks to the lack of more complex interlaced musical structures and language. There is almost no musical development, a slight change in structure sometimes, but nothing that would set a caesura. This means, it is not important for the listener where in the piece to start or stop listening. The locally varying song structures that do not change their global musical character at the same time provide the desired combination of inconspicuousness and interestingness for the listener.

Rhythm is an essential evidence for the comprehension of time (Kungel 2008). The intention of Ambient, though, is to make the listener forget about time. Hence, rhythm can only rarely be found in the majority of the analyzed pieces and, thus, tempo is not quite objectively determinable. The pure number of onsets per time unit cannot reflect the subjective impression of a mostly slow

[5]Tamm (1995), page 129.

tempo. This seems to be intended considering that fast tempi often mark emotional maxima which Ambient tries to avoid. Another important point is that the tempo almost never changes in an ambient piece, for it would also cause unwanted attention. Without a rhythm the search for a beat and measure is obsolete, too.

Differences in accentuation only occurred within little motifs, not least in order to give it a certain structure. Greater or even piece-wide changes in accentuation do not exist, only the single elements have different volumes. With this help, main voices and accompaniment can be distinguished.

On the part of the sound and instrumentation, Ambient seems to prefer sounds with hard, short attacks in the foreground, such as pianos, bells and marimbas, whereas smooth pad sounds with long attack phases accompany in the background and tend to blur. Release phases are always long and even further expanded by reverberation which recurs in every analyzed song. The album Ambient 4 also comes along with several noise, electronic and natural effect sounds.

Due to the loose coupling of parts, rests of up to ten seconds become a rather random but no arbitrary element. Because of the long releases and reverberation, background sounds blur into each other and even long rests are not absolutely silent.

### Conclusions

After a brief introduction to Ambient's expressive intentions we determined not only representative ambient songs from the often-called genre father Brian Eno but also found criteria for spectral analysis. As a result we identified several song elements which repeat in different intervals and are only synchronized by their onsets and chord harmonics, if at all. These elements featured the following properties:

- several tones with the same pitch and long attacks which are looped in independent but fixed cycles,
- chords that alternate in their positions but not in their tonal material,
- arpeggios on fixed, looped musical phrases that stop and restart in seemingly random intervals,
- looped short motifs built up from chord pitches,

- randomly appearing quiet electronic, natural or urban sounds, and
- random arpeggios over a fixed chord.

These will be revisited in section 3.5 in order to create a concept for algorithmically generated ambient music.

## 3.3 Music Generation

In contrast to nature and ambient noise like rustling wind in the trees, rushing sea or traffic noise, man-made music is clearly defined by beginning and end. If not, it repeats. Generative music, however, leaves that aspect behind. An aspect John Cage already tried to leave behind with his work (Collins & d'Escriván 2007). The first section told us that Ambient has the same properties and it does not matter when the listener starts listening. Hence, it is not surprising that Eno created a good portion of his pieces in a generative way with predefined rules (Eno 1996). He described generative music in an interview for the Wired News:

> "Ordinary music is like engineering, where everything's built according to a plan, and it's the same every time you play it. Generative music is more like gardening; you plant a seed, and it grows different every time you plant."[6]

It seems hard to algorithmically create music that does not only sound good but is also rich in content and emotionally intriguing. This is one big challenge of generative music.

The storage of non-generative music depends on the sampling rate and quantization, encoding and compression algorithms. With the modern storage technologies, capacity may not be an issue anymore, but if you want to store a continuous, non-repeating piece of music there are limits. For generative music, however, only the composition rules need to be stored and a finite number of sounds (if not synthesized, too). An algorithm of a few kilobytes can produce music that never repeats, assuming a sufficiently good (pseudo-)random number generator is included (Loy 2006).

Another advantage is that music that has been generated in this way can be controlled interactively even by amateurs and is flexible in temporal changes

[6] Schachtmann (2001).

(Berndt 2011). An ordinary score, by contrast, can be regarded as a fixed set of playing instructions. Performances of such scores tend to reproduction although there are exceptions (Potter 2002). An amateur would not be able to conduct and remodel a piece according to his own wishes. An algorithm, however, can be controlled by everybody, e.g. via a graphical user interface. Depending on the complexity of the music generator a few changes of input parameters can lead to completly different generated pieces, irrespective of the musical quality. There are three general approaches to interactive music (Berndt & Theisel 2008):

1. automatic arrangement of pre-composed material,
2. completely automatic composition of music and
3. hybrid approach, involving both pre-composed material and composition or adaptation algorithms

Nierhaus (2009) and Loy (2006) both provide an introduction to the paradigms of automatic music generation that have been used before. Those that are prospective candidates for interactive Ambient music generation are discussed in the following.

### 3.3.1 Musical Dice Games and Permutation

Musical dice games are based on random concatenation of pre-composed snippets. The tossing of a dice does not require any musical skills, the difficulty is to create musical snippets that fit together in any random combination. A possible procedure is to take a piece of music with a certain number of measures and create several variants for each in a way that all variants of a measure follow the same harmonic plan and feature similar melodic connections, thus, can be substituted by any other variant for this measure.

Johann Phillip Kirnberger (1767) was the first who provided musical dice games as a simple utility to create music. Other composers like Mozart and Haydn followed. It is not surprizing that musical dice games were invented in the classical era. With its strict aesthetic rules it was possible to create simple motifs for minuets and trios resulting in a well-formed classical piece in every variation (Loy 2006).

The strict approach to combine pre-composed material to a whole song is quite inflexible when it comes to customization and realtime interaction. But for Ambient with its different elements a musical dice game could be applicable for single elements, keeping the rest flexible.

Permutation can introduce more flexibility. It is the arrangement of a certain number of elements in a specific sequence. In a musical context these elements may be the notes of a motif or an arpeggio. So permutation may, for instance, change the note sequence of the arpeggio. This creates variations of the arpeggio without leaving the its musical boundaries (e.g., still keeping the same pitches). Permutation serves very well as an element in ambient music creation.

### 3.3.2 Markov Models

A Markov model is a probability model that was introduced in 1913 by the Russian mathematician Andrey Andreyevich Markov and is based on the so-called Markov chain (Brémaud 2008). The Markov chain defines the transition probability between symbols/states $\in \Sigma$. The initial state is $x_0$. The short notation $P(x_i|x_{i-1})$ respectively $P_{x_{i-1}x_i}$ describes such a transition probability from precedent state $x_{i-1}$ to the actual $x_i$. A Markov chain of the order/length $L$ can be represented as

$$P(x_1)\prod_{i=1}^{L} P_{x_{i-1}x_i} \qquad x_0,\ldots,x_L \in \Sigma$$

. A Markov model can also be represented by a transition matrix or a weighted directed graph (Kersting & Wakolbinger 2010). It is possible to train Markov models with musical note sequences. The order of the Markov model determines how many precedent notes are taken into account for the calculation of the next. The higher the order the higher the possibility of reproducing the original note sequence from the transition matrix (Loy 2006). Figure 3.4 demonstrates this effect with a German nursery rhyme.

Markov models of lower orders, even those trained by random melodies are very good at creating short recurrent motifs and phrases and, thus, are quite suitable for Ambient creation. The variations in the output sequence keeps the listener from getting bored by pure repetition. Additionally a user can be empowered to change the Markov model or its order during the music creation or even re-train it with new melodies on the fly.

### 3.3.3 Generative Grammars

Between 1955 and 1965 the American linguist Noam Chomsky developed outlines to formalize language. The object of the investigation is a well-formed

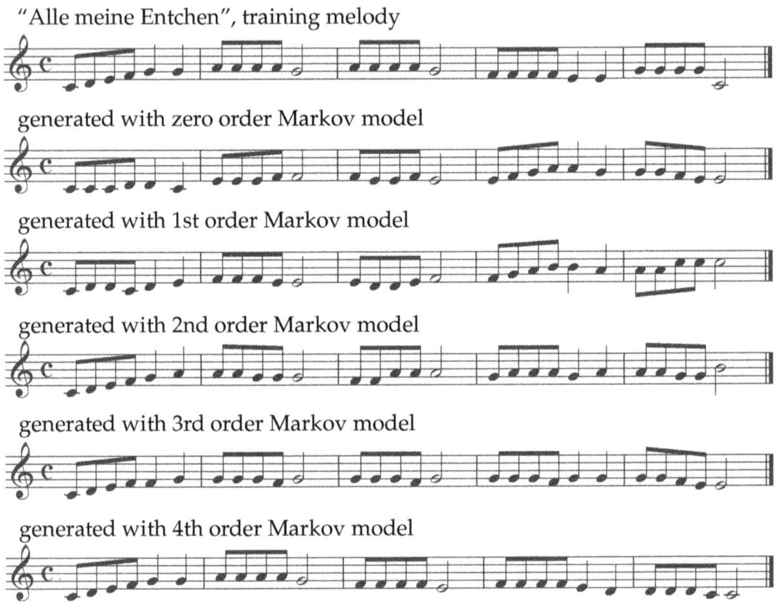


**Figure 3.4:** Melodies generated with Markov models of varying order.

sentence. A grammar that is able to generate only valid sentences is called *observationally adequate*. If it is also able to decide whether a sentence is valid, it is a *generative grammar* (Horrocks 1987). A grammar can be depicted by a set of symbols and production rules of all its sentences. Therefore constituents are iteratively substituted by others, until finally a lexicon replaces every constituent by a terminal symbol. Such a phrase structure grammar can be described as a 4-tuple $(V, \Sigma, S, P)$:

| | |
|---|---|
| $V$ | finite set of non-terminal symbols |
| $\Sigma$ | finite set of terminal symbols, $\Sigma \cap V = \emptyset$ and $\epsilon \in \Sigma$ |
| $S$ | start symbol $\in V$ |
| $P$ | set of production rules in the shape of $l \rightarrow r$ with $l \in (V \cup \Sigma)^+$ and $r \in (V \cup \Sigma)^*$ |

whereat $(V \cup \Sigma)^*$ describes the Kleene closure over $(V \cup \Sigma)$ and $(V \cup \Sigma)^+$ describes the positive closure over $(V \cup \Sigma)$ or $(V \cup \Sigma)^* \setminus \{\epsilon\}$. Starting with a non-terminal symbol, production rules are applied recursively until only terminal symbols remain on the right side. Chomsky also developed a hierarchy of grammars ascending in restriction and thus descending in generative capacity.

**Type-0 (unrestricted):** Arbitrarily long sequences of terminal symbols and non-terminal symbols can be on both sides of a production rule. The generative capacity is the highest within the Chomsky hierarchy, thus in the worst case the validation of a sentence may not be computed in finite time.

**Type-1 (context-sensitive):** The right side of the production rule must not be shorter than the left. This would decrease the decidability to an exponential complexity.

**Type-2 (context-free):** The left side of the production rule contains a single non-terminal symbol. The decision complexity is polynomial.

**Type-3 (regular):** A production rule must be of the shape $l \rightarrow \omega r$ or $l \rightarrow \omega$ with $l, r \in V$ and $\omega \in (\{\epsilon\} \cup \Sigma)$. The generative capacity is the smallest and the decidability linear.

A special representation of generative grammar is a transitional network. It is a set of finite automata in the shape of a directed graph. Nodes and edges describe the states and transitions of the automata. The edges are labelled with terminal symbols or non-terminal symbols. Every non-terminal symbol is represented by an own automaton. The traversal of a transitional network begins at a starting node and ends not until all non-terminal symbols have been replaced. Figure 3.5 shows a simple transitional network for creating a simple English sentence. Starting with a sentence as start automaton you may create for instance "the singer likes the conductor". If one augments the edges with commands, conditional jumps and subprograms it becomes an *augmented transitional network*, whose generative capacity bears resemblance to a type-0 grammar (Hoffmann 2011).

Since 1981 David Cope has been developing the algorithmic music system *Experiments in Musical Intelligence* (EMI) which is able to produce musical compositions according to predefined styles. EMI recombines existing material like a musical dice game. However, the decision about the concatenation is trained by an analysis model and is implemented by a complex augmented transitional

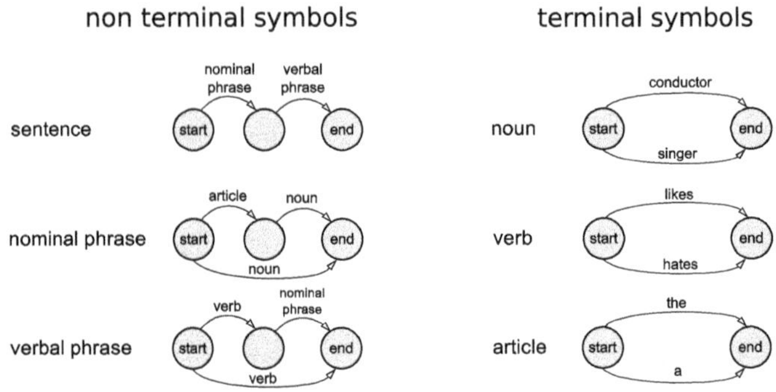


**Figure 3.5:** Transitional network for the generation of an English sentence. This figure ist based on Nierhaus (2009).

network. Cope's EMI shows that transitional networks are well suited to produce convincing musical material. Since the transition networks resemble the function of musical dice games, Loy (2006) calls them next-generation musical dice games. Our analysis shows that musical dice games are suitable for Ambient music creation, and so are transitional networks, plus they can be expanded with further conditions.

There are a bunch of possible applications for generative grammars regarding hierarchical musical structures, especially chord progression in Jazz or structuring of classical music (Nierhaus 2009). For the use in Ambient music, however, there are two special types of type-0 grammars suitable. *Augmented transitional networks* behave like advanced musical dice games and *fractal L-systems* use the recursiveness of generative grammars.

### 3.3.4 Fractals

Fractals are sets that feature one or more of these properties: defibration, porosity, complexity and self-similarity (Bronstein, Semendjajew, Musiol & Mühlig 2013). Self-similarity means, a smaller arbitrary part of the structure looks similar to the whole. Nature provides such structures almost everywhere in growing biological shapes like plants, coast-lines, crystallization, clouds, blood vessels, etc. 1990 botanist Aristid Lindenmayer developed a formal language based on the Chomsky grammars in order to represent the growth of plants, the L-

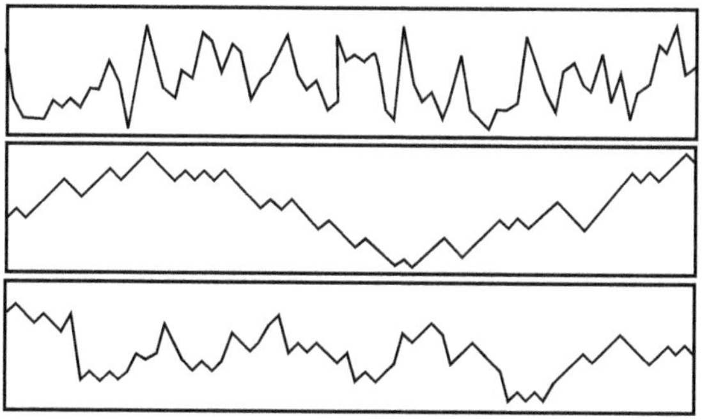

**Figure 3.6:** Examples of white (top), Brownian (middle) and pink noise (bottom). This figure is based on Nierhaus (2009).

systems (Prusinkiewicz & Lindenmayer 1990, Herrmann 1994). An L-system consists of an axiom (initial word) and a set of production rules according to a type-0 grammar. For instance is $a$ the axiom and

$$a \to b \quad \text{and} \quad b \to ba$$

are two production rules. The resulting string grows the following way:

| step | string |
|---|---|
| 1 | a |
| 2 | b |
| 3 | ba |
| 4 | bab |
| 5 | babba |
| 6 | babbabab |

Fractal noise includes several kinds of chaotic, fractal, random functions that differ in their spectral distribution. White noise is a stochastic process of uncorrelated random variables similar to a rolling dice. The ratio between amplitude and frequency distribution is frequency independent ($1/f^0$). Brown noise (Brownian movement), however, has correlated random values. Speaking of the dice metaphor an odd number means a pitch step up, an even number means a pitch step down. The spectral distribution is $1/f^2$. Pink noise is a compromise of both white and Brownian noise. The distribution is $1/f$. All three noises are exemplified in figur 3.6.

Prusinkiewicz (1986) demonstrated the mapping of an L-system-generated Hilbert curve onto a melody. Therefore, he took the distances of sequenced horizontal lines as tone intervals and the lengths as tones durations. This is but one example how to convert graphical interpretations of L-systems into musical ones.

According to Loy (2006) the secret of good music lies in the mixture of redundancy, which glues the music together, and surprise, which serves as a flavor enhancer. Fractals provide these very properties of unpredictability and intrinsic structural repetition. As described in section 3.2, Ambient pieces can build very well upon fractal structures.

## 3.4 Related Works

Ambient is a diverse genre that is hardly delimitable. Therefore it is no surprise that countless programs for Ambient music generation already exist. However, more than a few show that the genre itself is quite underestimated regarding its diversity. A common consensus seems to exist, that Ambient's only purpose is to relax the listener, often with the help of nature sounds. But speaking from the *furniture music* point of view Ambient music needs to cover any other emotional application domain as well. Ambient music played in an amusement park should not be the same as in a waiting room, an indoor swimming pool or in a shopping mall.

A number of different applications can be identified that generate interactive music and Ambient as well. This does not, however, imply any claim to completeness. Such applications are Orbits[7], Color Sounds[8], Ambient Mixer[9], Circuli and Otomata[10], Flux, SoundBow and SphereTones[11], Noatikl[12], and the apps Bloom, Trope, Scape, and Air[13] by Eno et al.

In this section we can only provide a condensed version of an analysis carried out by Müller (2013). There are five main criteria, the applications have been evaluated for:

[7] Vera (2011).
[8] Fehling (2013).
[9] `http://ambient-music.ambient-mixer.com/`, last accessed: Nov. 2014.
[10] EarSlap (2012, 2015).
[11] Binaura (2013*a*,*b*,*c*).
[12] Intermorphic Ltd. (2014).
[13] Eno & Chilvers (2011*a*,*b*, 2014), O'Neill & Chilvers (2012).

**Sound generation:** There are three groups. The first one uses recorded tones, the second synthesizes the tones and the third one is a hybrid where recorded material is modulated electronically.

**Composition:** What is the main principle that builds up the musical structure?

**Finiteness:** Is the generated material repeated after a still perceptible time period, e.g. 24 hours?

**Level of interaction** How much influence can the user exert to the music generation?

**Purposeful control of the character of expression:** Are there meta-parameters that enable control on an emotional level?

Table 3.1 compares all evaluated applications according to the five criteria. Most apps are based on an innovative, graphically linked sound composition. Thus, they intentionally forgo ways of interaction in order to keep the user interface clean and simple so that users are not overcharged. Only Noatikl resembles a patch programming environment, which provides full interaction but sacrifices clarity. Regardless of the level of interaction, none of the analyzed applications provides a purposeful control of the character of expression. The approach presented in the remainder of this chapter, by contrast, has its focus on full interactivity in the first step creating as many parameters as possible. The second step is to condense the confusing number of input parameters to precise emotional expression controls, in order to make it simple again on a meta level.

## 3.5 Interactive Ambient Music Generator

During his talk about generative music, Brian Eno asked the question who the composer of a generative piece may be:

> "You never know who made it. With this generative music that I played you, am I the composer? Are you if you buy the system the composer? Is Jim Coles and his brother who wrote the software the composer? – Who actually composes music like this? Can you describe it as composition exactly when you don't know what it's going to be?"[14]

[14] Eno (1996).

| Application | Type * | Sound Generation | Composition | ∞ | Realtime Interaction |
|---|---|---|---|---|---|
| Reactable-likes | SA | synth. | patching environment | – | >2 |
| Bloom | SA | synth. | sound points | ✓ | 2 |
| Trope | SA | synth. | sound curves | ✓ | 2 |
| Air | SA | synth. | keys | – | 1 |
| Otomata | WA | synth. | cellular automata | – | 2 |
| Circuli | WA | synth. | sound points | – | 1 |
| Orbits | SA | synth. | physical sim. | ✓ | 2 |
| Color Sounds | SA | synth. | color, camera | ✓ | 1 |
| Ambient-Mixer | WA | sampled | sample-mix | ✓ | 2 |
| Flux | SA | synth. | sound curve | ✓ | 1 |
| SoundBow | SA | synth. | sound curves | – | 2 |
| SphereTones | SA | synth. | synth-mix | – | 2 |
| Noatikl | SA | synth. | patching environment | ✓ | 6 |

* SA = smartphone app; WA = web application
** level of realtime interaction: 0 (none), 1 (very low), 2 (low), 3(middle), 4(high), 5 (very high), 6 (fully interactive)

**Table 3.1:** Comparison of the evaluated Ambient music generators. None of them offers control over the emotional character of expression.

This question is warranted if it comes to a generative system with a high degree of freedom, that cannot be controlled precisely. The concept developed in this section, however, has a clear answer. It provides a fixed Ambient infrastructure flavored with random events, which are influenced by user interaction. Thus, the user keeps the composition under control.

The following section covers the conception of a simple synthesizer and generation techniques derived from our analyses in sections 3.2 and 3.3. After introducing basic concepts of sound synthesis, section 3.5.2 introduces our new composition algorithm. Interaction interfaces at both elementary and meta-level create the foundation for selective control of the character of expressions in section 3.6.

### 3.5.1 Sound Synthesis

It is the periodicity of the wave function that separates a harmonic sound from noise. This very property allows us to perceive different pitches. Noise, however, is not associated with a specific pitch due to its chaotic nature. The human auditory sensation is logarithmic in many regards. An exponential increase of frequency is perceived as a linear increase in pitch. With the help of hair cells the ear is able to distinguish the mixed frequencies of a sound in a range from approximately 20Hz to 20kHz. The deepest frequency of a tone is sensed as the fundamental frequency. The natural overtones (harmonics) are multiples of the fundamental. There are several exceptions to this, that should be noted, e.g. the relationship between pitch and amplitude and missing fundamental illusions. These will not be further considered in this work. For more details please refer to Schenk & Rigoll (2010).

The sensation of consonance or dissonance of pitch intervals may be subjective, contextual and culturally influenced.[15] However, octave (doubling of reference frequency $f_R$) and perfect fifth $\left(\frac{3}{2}f_R\right)$ are perceived similarly among all cultures, because they are the first two intervals in the natural series of overtones. That is why constructors of musical tuning systems orient themselves on them. In the western world the equal temperament is the most common tuning system. Another widely spread tuning system is the natural pentatonic scale which is constructed solely from perfect fifths and octaves (Loy 2006). These tuning systems will both be implemented in the Ambient music generator.

#### Synthesis Techniques

In order to gain full control over the generated tones, a completely synthetic, i.e. not sample-based, sound generation procedure is created. A synthesizer is a tool that generates tones and noises electronically by patching several unit generators and transformations (Eimert & Humpert 2007). There are several ways of creating the spectrum of a sound. Here, we focus on additive and subtractive synthesis.

*Additive synthesis* creates a complex sound by adding partial tones. This is based on the Fourier synthesis. Joseph Fourier discovered that every however-complex periodical oscillation (tone) can be built from the sum of sine functions with cer-

[15] Busoni and Schönberg, two great musicians and musical theorists of the 19th and 20th century even denied dissonance any musical reality, see Eimert & Humpert (2007), page 67.

tain frequencies (integer multiples of the fundamental frequency), amplitudes and phase angles. Most common waveforms are (Loy 2007) the following.

$$f(t) = \sum_{k=0}^{N-1} \frac{1}{2k+1} sin(2\pi(2k+1)t) \qquad N > 0 \quad \text{rectangle}$$

$$f(t) = \sum_{k=0}^{N-1} \frac{1}{(2k+1)^2} cos(2\pi(2k+1)t) \qquad N > 0 \quad \text{triangle}$$

$$f(t) = \sum_{k=1}^{N} \frac{(-1)^{k+1}}{k} sin(2\pi kt) \qquad N > 0 \quad \text{sawtooth}$$

The concept of additive synthesis can be understood more generally. It is not limited to the use of sine signals and integer frequencies which opens the concept for inharmonic spectra as demonstrated by the TouchNoise interface in chapter 2 of this book.

With *subtractive synthesis*, a complex frequency spectrum is filtered. To achieve changes in timbre over time the filter cutoff can be modulated. Time-dependent functions (signals) can be used to *modulate* further sound parameters such as frequency, amplitude and phase.

A great variety of further synthesis approaches exists. Our further descriptions will, however, focus on the approach that is implemented in the Ambient music generator. This relatively simple synthesizer served as a means for cresting the typical sound characteristics observed in the analysis and for testing of different scales and tuning systems. In a realworld application scenario this synthesizer would be replayed by external modules such as VST plugins that allow a more complex and versatile design of musical and effect sounds.

### Envelope

A musical sound signal passes several amplitude phases which differ in amplitude and duration depending on the instrument. The most common envelope model (ADSR) is shown in figure 3.7. The settling time ranges from silence to a maximum (attack), in order to decline (decay) to a constant energy level (sustain level). The amplitude now stays stable (sustain time) until the tone is released and declines to silence (Loy 2006). Attack and release are very important phases because they ultimately influence the listening experience. An extremely short attack or release would lead to an uncomfortable snapping or popping sound in the beginning or end of the tone. To avoid such effects in electronic sound

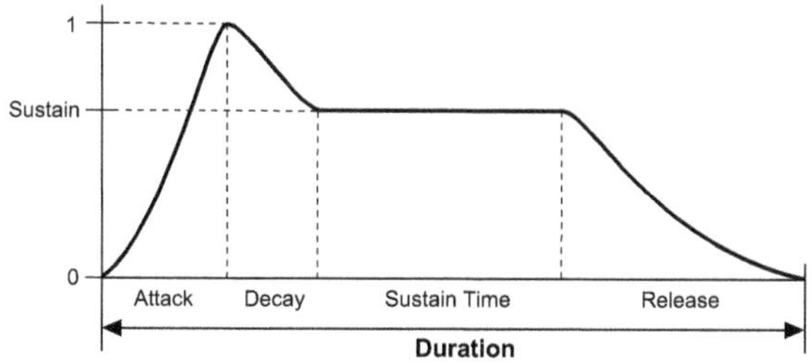


**Figure 3.7:** The ADSR model of volume envelope.

synthesis, envelope functions are multiplied with the generated sound signal. Envelope functions and other modulator signals (e.g., low frequency oscillators, LFOs) can be used to control not only amplitudes but also other sound generating units, e.g. the parameters of a filter.

### Concept of an Interactive Synthesizer

The synthesizer features a modular design and builds a circuit of unit generators. A bank of sine waves serves as carrier signals and creates the partials of the whole tone. To create the overtones of the fundamental, frequency factors can be multiplied with it on every carrier. The carriers themselves are modulated in frequency and amplitude by connecting their inputs with the outputs of arbitrarily shaped modulator units. A typical modulator is a sine which creates a tremolo when applied to the amplitude and a vibrato when applied to frequency (Eimert & Humpert 2007, Loy 2007). The inputs of the modulators each get an envelope, in order to control the effect of a modulator on a temporal manner. The circuit with modulators and carriers is shown in figure 3.8. The red coloured fundamental input and the gate input are not used before runtime.

All carrier signals are then added, filtered and modulated with another envelope. The filter parameters can be controlled by modulators and envelopes as well. Finally, the whole tone is processed by a flanger and a simple reverberator (Howe 1975). In figure 3.9 the whole synthesizer is depicted. Table 3.2 recapitulates almost all parameters for timbre creation and their runtime interaction. All parameter settings can be stored and recalled at runtime by storing its input parameters.

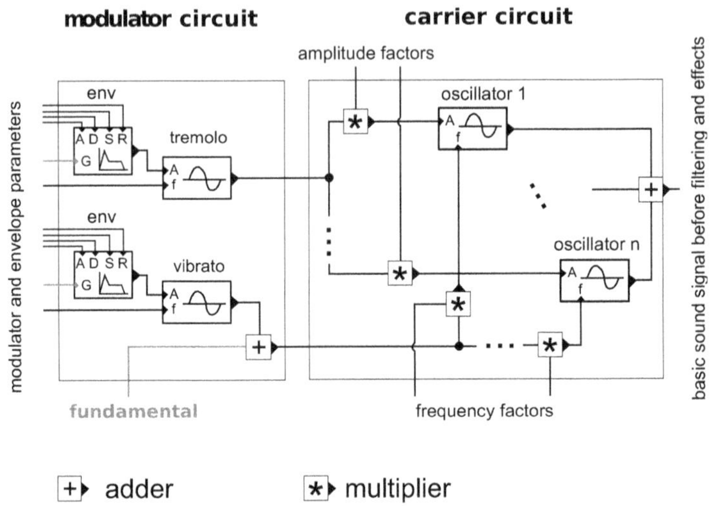


**Figure 3.8:** The sound synthesis patch of the Ambient music generator.

### 3.5.2 Composition

As determined in section 3.2, an Ambient song consists of several different, independent and often repetitive musical elements, that may be loosely linked by the tonal material of an underlying chord (mostly only one chord for the whole piece) and metrical synchrony (rhythm, respectively). In order to implement these links, all elements play tones from the same main chord. If two elements have the same tempo, their onsets are synchronous. This is provided by a master tempo that is measured in beats per minute. Every beat can be thought as a beginning time slot. The elements themselves have their own tempi that are linked with a factor each to that master tempo, called element beats. If the user wants, element beats can be unlinked or relinked to the master level beat. Fol-

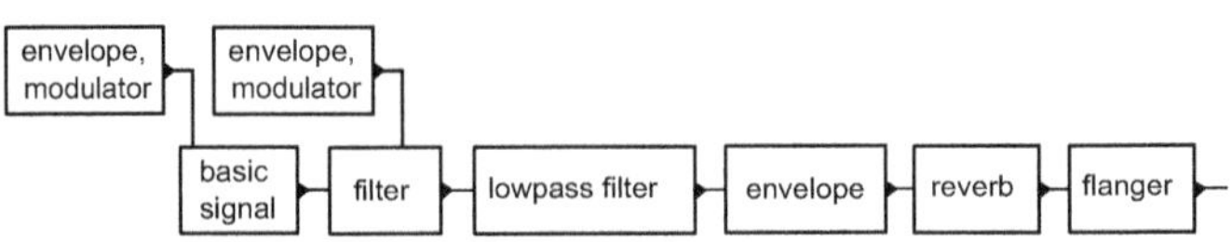


**Figure 3.9:** Filtering and effects section of the sound generation.

| Unit | Input Parameter | On The Fly Interaction |
|---|---|---|
| carrier | fundamental | ✓ |
| | amplitude, frequency factor | – |
| carrier modulator | amplitude, frequency | – |
| carrier envelope | gate, attack, decay, sustain, release | ✓ |
| modulator envelope | attack, decay, sustain, release | – |
| | gate | ✓ |
| filter | cut-off frequency, filter steepness | – |
| filter modulator | amplitude, frequency | – |
| lowpass filter | cutoff frequency, filter steepness | ✓ |
| reverb | number of repeats | ✓ |
| | repetition time, reduction factor | ✓ |
| | amplitude damping factor | ✓ |
| flanger | frequency of phase shifting | – |
| | amplitude of phase shifting | – |

**Table 3.2:** An overview of the Ambient music generator's sound synthesis parameters.

lowing the example of Brian Eno's Ambient 1 track "1/1", elements may play their musical phrase for a certain (random) amount of element beats and then rest independently for a random amount of element beats before they continue with a new musical phrase. These two random periods can be delimited by the user. After every rest phrases are generated again. Fixed loops are avoided this way. Each element features a series of further parameters.

**Volume** determines the element's loudness in the mix of all elements.

**Tempo** controls the number of element beats per meta level beat.

**Maximum length of phrases and rests between phrases** determines the pace of the "musical breathing".

**Amplitude envelope** as described in the previous section.

**Tone length** is either fixed, or the tone is held until the next one.

**Conclusion** The last played tone before a break has a longer release in order to emphasize it acoustically.

**Maximum deviation from meta rhythm** is a factor that limits random numbers which shift every onset of a tone played by this element. The default factor zero means that there is no shift and the onsets of that element are synchronized with its element beat.

**Reverberator** with repetition time, number of repetitions, damping factor, and shortening factor.

**Lowpass filter** , cuts off high frequencies, thus damps shrill timbres. The user decides whether to control the cutoff frequency manually or let it change autonomously through Brownian noise. The third possibility is to link the cutoff frequency to the pitch of another element for a subtle connection.

**Frequency factor** can get elements out of tune (for selective beat frequencies or dissonances), create specific mixtures (e.g., a fifth), or change the octave transposition of the element.

**Note value** gives the choice between fixed note values (quarter notes) or varied values created by a Markov model, that is trained with several input melodies. The order of the Markov chain and the training set can be changed on the fly.

Every element contains at least one synthesizer instrument (figure 3.9) with each one having its own stored timbre (set of input parameters). If an element contains several instruments, random numbers are generated for each of them separately. All other parameters are the same for all instruments within the element. The Ambient song player instantiates five elements:

### Yoyo Element

This monophonic element is an arpeggiator. Given, for instance, a main chord with pitches $C\ D\ E\ F\ G$, the yoyo element initially plays the sequence

$$C\,D\,E\,F\,G\,F\,E\,D\,C\,D\,E\,F\ldots$$

To vary this sequence, the main chord can be permuted automatically.

### Bass Element

This element has two monophonic instances of an instrument, even though the bass is a monophonic voice. The two instances allow for two succeeding bass tones to overlap without the unwanted voice stealing effect. The notes are chosen randomly from the set of chord notes and transposed into bass pitch range.

### Markov Element

This monophonic instrumented element uses a Markov model to create recurrent, varying patterns/motifs in the tone sequence of the main chord and thus provides a quasi-melody. The model is trained with a set of melodies. The model can be interactively retrained with an arbitrary combination of stored melodies. Also the order of the Markov model can be chosen by the user. Furthermore, the user can choose, if the Markov chain only produces tones within the main chord or non-chord tones as well. Keys of the training melodies are also stored. The user may choose melodies that already musically relate to the main chord.

### Chord Element

This element operates four instances of monophonic instruments that play four random tones from the main chord in random octave transpositions. Due to every instrument having its own rests, it is not sure that all four tones are played simultaneously. The maximum pitch range can be adjusted by the user. At level 0 the played chord lies within an octave. A maximum arpeggio time can be controlled as well. If it is set greater than zero, the chord is played arpeggiated and the note sequence becomes an important aspect.

### Samples

This element operates three instruments (or tracks) and plays a random combination of selectable sound samples. These can be of any noise or sound, although this element should primarily contribute nature sounds, animal sounds and urban noises into the ambient song. The sample element is no part of the synthesizer, but the sample units may also be modulated, filtered etc. like the other elements.

#### Master

Besides the parameters which can be controlled for each element at runtime individually, there are also global parameters.

**Scale:** sequence of semitone steps that define the main scale, for instance:

| | |
|---|---|
| major | 2 2 1 2 2 2 1 |
| minor | 2 1 2 2 1 2 2 |

**Tonic:** fundamental pitch of the chosen scale.

**Octave index:** of the tonic, transposes the scale.

**Chord:** selection of 5 positions within the chosen scale. The advantage of this method is the easy way of transposing and changing scales on the fly without the need to change each chord position.

**Song tempo:** in beats per minute (bpm).

**Volume, rest length, phrase length, attack, decay, sustain, release:** all factors to the equally named element parameters, e.g. a meta volume of 0.5 would halve all the element volumes.

**Filter, reverb, flanger:** after all instrument outputs of all elements have been added, the resulting signal is finally processed by a global lowpass filter, a reverb and a flanger.

## 3.6 The Player Module

The player module is a high-level interface that allows for the complex control of the underlying Ambient music algorithm. It provides scripting features, handles all the input parameters and features the exploration of the musical potentials of the algorithm, by allowing to store and load different sets of input parameters regarding their resulting expressive musical character.

Figure 3.10 shows the whole synthesis patch with all instrument instances. The resulting signal is finally multiplied by a factor to control the master volume. The program generating the song needs to control the gates of all envelopes and send impulses to play tones. Simply changing the input parameters leads to a countless amount of different Ambient song compositions, that can be stored

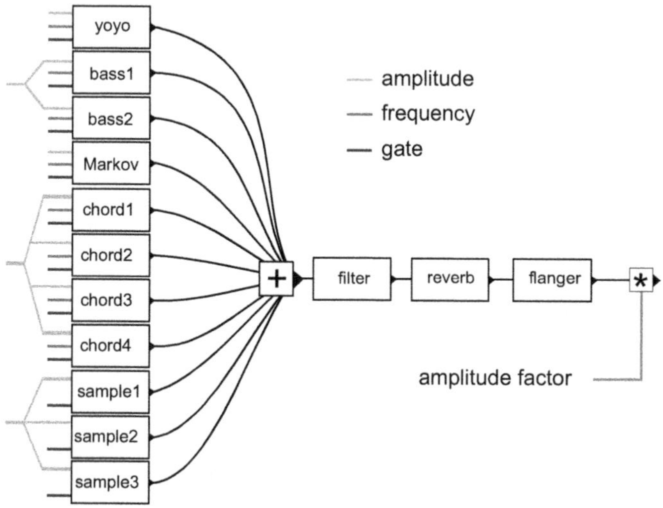


**Figure 3.10:** All instruments (synthesizer instances) of all elements of the Ambient music generator.

and loaded at runtime. A priori there is no musically meaningful combination of parameters, so in the beginning it is up to the user to create and store a set of songs. Another feature allows the user to record and store the audio output created in this way. The concept in the current version does not yet allow dynamic changes in the way the elements play. Songs generated this way may be ambient and do not repeat (real random numbers assumed), but are restricted to a narrow musical range and could appear monotonous and boring after some time. To avoid this, several dynamic features are added, which automatically vary the static parameters. The frequency and the amount of these changes can be chosen by the user.

### Dynamic Feature

The song parameters change randomly according to Brownian motion, yet in a way that does not change the character of the piece too much, in order to avoid inconsistencies in the listening experience. To say it with Eno's metaphor: the same Ambient piece (in this case a specific parameter combination) can grow like different plants from the same seed (Schachtmann 2001). With every interactively adjustable time step

- the maximum pause and phrase lengths are either extended or shortened,
- a random tone of the main chord is by the next lower scale position with 33% probability,
- tempi at element level are increased or decreased by factor 1.05 with 33% probability,
- every amplitude of all elements is either increased or decreased by factor 1.1 with 33% probability,
- all filter cutoffs change according to Brownian motion,
- permutation is enabled for the yoyo element,
- the pitch range of the chord element is decreased or increased with 33% probability, and
- the Markov element is retrained with a random combination of stored training melodies.

The factors were chosen empirically, so that changes are slightly perceivable, but not too striking.

#### Bridge

Instead of replacing all parameters when it comes to loading a stored song, the values can be gradually interpolated between current and target values. So one song slowly morphs into another. The user may now choose the coarseness of the interpolation. The higher the coarseness, the longer it takes until the parameters reach the target values of the loaded song. If the user disables the bridge feature during this interpolation process, a new hybrid song is generated and can be stored as well.

#### Chaotic

The chaotic feature is more a gimmick than a serious function. Based on white noise all parameters get a completely random value with every interactively adjustable time step. This feature, however, may be used to find new songs.

| Joy | Grief | Unease |
| --- | --- | --- |
| fast tempo,<br>huge increasing intervals,<br>metrically synchronized instr.,<br>short tones,<br>major keys | slow tempo,<br>short increasing intervals,<br>minor keys,<br>quiet, long damped tones,<br>disharmony,<br>isolated voice | irregular rhythm,<br>long beats, dissonances,<br>disharmony,<br>long reverberation,<br>high noise ratio, atonal noises |

| Relaxation | Threat/danger |
| --- | --- |
| quiet, very long, blurring tones,<br>long reverberation,<br>damped tones,<br>pentatonic | loud, short bass,<br>fast tempo,<br>tremolo,<br>tones 1 octave higher,<br>loud tones,<br>long beats,<br>shrill timbre,<br>frequent volume changes,<br>irregular rhythm,<br>minor keys |

**Table 3.3:** Settings for emotional coloring, based on Kungel (2008) and Liu (2010).

### Emotional Coloring

Emotions emerging from music are extremely subjective. Clear relations between musical features and emotions are thus not determined easily. The concept supports two approaches. The first one applies empirical knowledge about the emotional effect of certain musical features. Table 3.3 gives an overview of the stylistic devices implemented in the player module, based on Kungel (2008) and movie analyst Liu (2010).

These musical devices are quite rudimental and cover only a general social consensus. The second approach solves this problem by learning the subjective sensation of the user. Every time the user creates and saves a new song, he may tag it with an emotional class. A song then belongs to one or more classes, into which the user puts it. Whenever an emotional class is selected in the dynamics feature, a random song from this particular category is chosen and its parameters are taken as target values. To avoid a simple reproduction of the chosen song, the meta parameters as well as all individual parameters of all elements are left unchanged. The user, however, may choose to adopt the main chord and the instrumentation. An advanced feature may add all newly tagged emotion classes to the dynamics feature.

The first approach is suitable for the initial phase of the player, when there are no or only few stored songs in the player's repertoire. The more songs are stored and tagged, the more reasonable the second approach gets. Thus, the variety of the Ambient song generator grows with the subjective user input and get more and more diverse.

### Scheduler

Despite the introduced dynamics feature, the concept yet demands the presence and interaction of the user in order to, for instance, switch emotional categories, or change the main chord after a while. To overcome this demand, a scheduler has been added to the concept. It enables the creation of a chronologic queue of song events that is processed by the player module at runtime. These events can represent any change of any parameter in the whole player (not only those that determine a song). Events can happen simultaneously and sequentially. A queue or schedule can be looped, stored, loaded, deleted, and also cancelled during its processing. A song event consists of three components: (1) the parameter to be changed, (2) its new target value and (3) the time distance to the preceding event. A simple queue could look like this:

$$
\begin{aligned}
&[\text{Song} \mid \mathit{mySong} \mid 10] \longrightarrow \\
&[\text{yoyo Permutation} \mid \mathit{TRUE} \mid 7] \longrightarrow \\
&[\text{yoyo Permutation Frequency} \mid 20 \mid 0] \longrightarrow \\
&[\text{Dynamics} \mid \mathit{Joy} \mid 600] \longrightarrow \\
&[\text{Master Attack} \mid \mathit{random} \mid 120] \circlearrowleft
\end{aligned}
$$

This queue describes the following: ten seconds after the start, the song named *mySong* is loaded. Seven seconds later permutation is enabled for the yoyo element. Immediately after that (zero seconds later) the permutation will change every 20 tones. After six minutes the dynamics changes to *Joy*. Additional two minutes later the master attack is set to a random value. The queue then loops and starts at the beginning.

This functionality becomes most interesting, if in the first event a random song is loaded or if events could also affect the queue itself. The scheduler now represents a recursive transitional network which replaces non-terminals (events) by specific instances (musical output). Thus, the same queue is able to produce a variety of meta songs.

## 3.7 Discussion

This chapter introduced a concept for generating interactive Ambient music based on the results of the analyses in section 3.2 and the discussion of generative paradigms in section 3.3. A modular synthesizer was the first part of the concept. The unit generator patch provides the creation of different instrument timbres depending on the combinations of input parameters. This way it is not needed to change the structure of the system when creating a new timbre at runtime, but it also means that the system is not scalable. The timbres can be stored and loaded at runtime. The described sound synthesis is, however, limited, especially regarding the provided polyphony and timbres. If more is needed, the music playback should be streamed into external synthesizers (e.g., via MIDI). This functionality could be a gainful future extension of the system.

The Ambient music generator, so far, works with five musical elements with altogether eleven instruments. All instruments have their own assignable timbre, except of the three instruments of the sample element, which play recorded samples from the sample database (urban, nature and electronic sounds and noises). All elements primarily play on the same main chord and are adapted to synchronization by tempo. The Markov element also provides non-chord tones, if desired. Each element has its individual way to play the five tones of the main chord, rest and continue independently after a random but interactively adjustable time. The yoyo and chord element use permutations. The Markov element uses on-the-fly-trainable Markov chains to generate Ambient song structures. The bass and sample elements decorate the song musically. All elements are locally and globally controllable via diverse parameters at runtime. The combination of the parameters constitutes an Ambient song that can be saved and loaded.

A song generated this way may be non-repetitive—provided randomized play parameters—but musically monotonous. To address this problem features are added to design dynamic song structures and selectively influence the emotional character of expression. Therefore, two approaches are devised in order to build a complex emotional repertoire over time, one fixed and empiric, the other flexible and subjective.

On the meta level, complex song progressions can be created by the user via an event scheduler that processes the event queue like a generative grammar. These schedules can also be saved and loaded. Now, the user does not need to interact all the time with the program, in order to create longterm song progressions. The

| Component | Interaction At Runtime | Function |
|---|---|---|
| Timbre Tester | test, save, load timbre | create timbre |
| yoyo element | permutation, frequency of permutation | play 1 instrument |
| bass element | — | play 2 instruments |
| Markov element | select a set of training melodies, order of Markov chain | play 1 instrument |
| chord element | arpeggio time, pitch range | play 4 instruments |
| sample element | select a set of samples, frequency of played samples | play samples |
| all elements | volume*, ADSR-envelope*, max. phrase time* & break time*, tempo*, lowpass parameter*, reverb parameter*, tone length*, frequency factor change timbre, hold tone, Markov chain for pitches | |
| meta | factor for every *-interaction, tag, save, load, delete song, start, stop recording, start ,pause ,stop player | control player & elements |
| song dynamics | static, dynamic, chaotic, happy, sad, threatening, relaxed, bizarre | dynamics, expr. of movements |
| scheduler | save, load, loop queue, start, stop queue | create event, event queue |

**Table 3.4:** All components of Ambient song player, its functions and ways of interaction

produced output signal can be recorded. Table 3.4 summarizes all components of the concept and their interaction possibilities.

Due to its realtime interactive features and the purposeful control of the character of expression the designed player is suitable for the musical scoring of interactive environments like open-world games. In those games the world is often created algorithmically with randomized parameters and it is potentially infinite. A normal and finite music score in this infinite world and undetermined playing time would repeat rather quickly and bore or even annoy the player after a while. The on-the-fly generated Ambient music, however, would never repeat and could adapt its emotional character to the game context (daytime, spatial location, gameplay mode, etc.). The advantage of the once initialized, predetermined but non-scalable unit generator architecture is, that it demands only a fixed amount of computing resources and does not become a bottleneck later.

## 3.8 Conclusion and Future Perspectives

When it comes to composition and performance, non-generative music is limited to the physical presence of competent musicians and their acoustic or electronic instruments. This kind of music is unique, not easy to reproduce and restricted in time and storage. Interaction with the listener is nearly impossible. All these disadvantages are addressed by generative music with its algorithmic composition and creation. Thus, the aim of this chapter was to design a concept for creating interactive Ambient music.

Section 3.2 gave a brief insight into the history of the genre Ambient and identified its specific properties. Section 3.3 discussed several paradigms of algorithmic music generation which are suitable for Ambient music. A research of existing Ambient music generators revealed their lack of interaction on an emotional level. This is where section 3.5 ties in. The results from these sections were used to design an interactive Ambient music generator and player that is able to purposefully control the character of expression on various musical levels.

Despite the many functions the design already offers, its musical quality is still in its infancy. The introduction of further dependencies among the elements may enhance their musical coherence. Further knowledge, for instance from the movie and game industry may refine the existing emotional categories and increase their quality. Furthermore, the concept so far focussed on the musical generation and its parameters, not, however, on the interface by which it is controlled. The sheer amount of parameters and their meaning would overstrain musically inexperienced users. A good starting point would be the design of user roles and their level of interaction to provide the corresponding parts of the interface.

# Bibliography


Berndt, A. (2011), *Musik für interaktive Medien: Arrangement- und Interpretationstechniken*, Verlag Dr. Hut, Munich, Germany.

Berndt, A. (2014), Ambiente Musik zur Vertonung immersiver interaktiver Medien, *in* Institut für immersive Medien, ed., 'Jahrbuch immersiver Medien 2014: Klänge, Musik und Soundscapes', Schüren Verlag, Fachhochschule Kiel, Germany, pp. 95–105.

Berndt, A. & Theisel, H. (2008), Adaptive Musical Expression from Automatic Realtime Orchestration and Performance, *in* U. Spierling & N. Szilas, eds, 'Interactive Digital Storytelling (ICIDS) 2008', Springer, Erfurt, Germany, pp. 132–143. LNCS 5334.

Binaura (2013*a*), 'Flux', app on Google play.
**URL:** *http://www.binaura.net/stc/wrx/flux/*

Binaura (2013*b*), 'SoundBow', app on Google play.
**URL:** *http://www.binaura.net/stc/wrx/soundbow/*

Binaura (2013*c*), 'SphereTones', app on Google play.

Brémaud, P. (2008), *Markov Chains: Gibbs Fields, Monte Carlo Simulation, and Queues*, Vol. 31 of *Texts in Applied Mathematics*, corrected edn, Springer Verlag, New York, NY USA.

Bronstein, I. N., Semendjajew, K. A., Musiol, G. & Mühlig, H. (2013), *Taschenbuch der Mathematik*, 9th corrected edn, Edition Harri Deutsch, Verlag Europa-Lehrmittel, Haan-Gruiten, Germany.

Collins, N. & d'Escriván, J., eds (2007), *The Cambridge Companion to Electronic Music*, Cambridge University Press, Cambridge, UK.

EarSlap (2012), 'Circuli—Generative Ambient Sound Instrument', app on iTunes. version 1.0.
**URL:** *http://www.earslap.com/page/circuli.html*

EarSlap (2015), 'Otomata—Generative Musical Sequencer', app on iTunes. version 1.5.
**URL:** *http://www.earslap.com/page/otomata.html*

Eimert, H. & Humpert, H. U. (2007), *Das Lexikon der elektronischen Musik*, Vol. 2 of *Bosse Musik Paperback*, 3rd edn, Gustav Bosse Verlag, Regensburg, Germany.

Eno, B. (1996), 'Generative Music: Evolving metaphors, in my opinion, is what artists do', *In Motion Magazine* (July issue).

Eno, B. & Chilvers, P. (2011*a*), 'Bloom', Opal Limited. app on iTunes, v2.1.1.

Eno, B. & Chilvers, P. (2011*b*), 'Trope', Opal Limited. app on iTunes, v1.2.

Eno, B. & Chilvers, P. (2014), 'Scape', Opal Limited. app on iTunes, v1.1.

Fehling, K. (2013), 'Color Sounds: Generative music', app on Google play.
**URL:** *http://androidideas.org/colorsounds/*

Herrmann, D. (1994), *Algorithmen für Chaos und Fraktale*, Addison-Wesley, Bonn, Germany.

Hoffmann, D. W. (2011), *Theoretische Informatik*, 2nd updated edn, Carl Hanser Verlag, Munich, Germany.

Holmes, T. (2012), *Electronic and Experimental Music: Technology, Music, and Culture*, 4th edn, Routledge, Taylor & Francis, New York, NY, USA.

Horrocks, G. (1987), *Generative Grammar*, Longman Linguistics Library, Longman Publishing Group, Routledge, Taylor & Francis, London, UK.

Howe, H. S. (1975), *Electronic Music Synthesis: Concepts, Facilities, Techniques*, W. W. Norton & Co., New York, NY, USA.

Intermorphic Ltd. (2014), 'Noatikl Generative Music Composer and MIDI-Generator System', app on iTunes. version 2.7.22.
**URL:** *http://intermorphic.com/noatikl/*

Kersting, G. & Wakolbinger, A. (2010), *Elementare Stochastik*, 2nd revised edn, Birkhäuser, Springer, Basel, Switzerland.

Kirnberger, J. P. (1767), *Der allezeit fertige Polonaisen und Menuetten Komponist*, G. L. Winter, Berlin, Germany. trans.: The Ever Ready Composer of Polonaises and Minuets.

Kungel, R. (2008), *Filmmusik für Filmemacher: Die richtige Musik zum besseren Film*, 2nd edn, Dpunkt Verlag, Edition Mediabook, Heidelberg, Germany.

Liu, G. (2010), *Die Macht der Filmmusik: Zum Verhältnis von musikalischem Ausdruck und Emotionsvermittlung im Film*, Vol. 19 of *Wissenschaftliche Beiträge aus dem Tectum Verlag, Reihe Psychologie*, Tectum Verlag, Marburg, Germany.

Loy, G. (2006), *Musimathics: The Mathematical Foundations of Music*, Vol. 1, MIT Press, Cambridge, Massachusets.

Loy, G. (2007), *Musimathics: The Mathematical Foundations of Music*, Vol. 2, MIT Press, Cambridge, Massachusets.

Milkowski, B. (1983), 'Brian Eno: Excursions in the Electronic Environment', *Down Beat: The Contemporary Music Magazine* (June issue).

Miller, R. (1998), 'Riven: The Soundtrack', Cyan, Inc.

Müller, M. (2013), Interaktive Ambiente Musik, Diploma thesis, Technische Universität Dresden, Faculty of Computer Science, Dresden, Germany.

Nierhaus, G. (2009), *Algorithmic Composition: Paradigms of Automated Music Generation*, Springer Verlag, Wien, Austria.

O'Neill, S. & Chilvers, P. (2012), 'Air', Opal Limited. app on iTunes, v1.3.

Potter, K. (2002), *Four Musical Minimalists: La Monte Young, Terry Riley, Steve Reich, Philip Glass*, Music in the Twentieth Century, revised edn, Cambridge University Press, Cambridge, UK.

Prusinkiewicz, P. (1986), Score generation with L-systems, *in* 'Proc. of the Int. Computer Music Conf. (ICMC) 1986', Royal Conservatory of Music, Den Haag, Netherlands, pp. 455–457.

Prusinkiewicz, P. & Lindenmayer, A. (1990), *The Algorithmic Beauty of Plants*, The Virtual Laboratory, Springer Verlag, New York, NY, USA.

Schachtmann, N. (2001), *New Eno Music Gets 'Generative'*. quoted by the author in Wired News.

Schenk, J. & Rigoll, G. (2010), *Mensch-Maschine-Kommunikation: Grundlagen von sprach- und bildbasierten Benutzerschnittstellen*, Springer Verlag, Berlin, Heidelberg, Germany.

Schulze, H. (2000), *Das aleatorische Spiel: Erkundung und Anwendung der nicht-intenionalen Werkgenese im 20. Jahrhundert*, Wilhelm Fink Verlag, Paderborn, Germany.

Soule, J. (2011), 'The Elder Scrolls V: Skyrim Original Game Soundtrack', Bethesda Softworks.

Tamm, E. (1995), *Brian Eno: His Music And The Vertical Color Of Sound*, Da Capo Press, Boston, MA.

Vera, B. (2011), 'Orbits—Generative Music', app on Google play.

Axel Berndt

Chapter 4

# Formalizing Expressive Music Performance Phenomena

**Abstract** What is the curve shape of a ritardando? How loud is forte and how does a decrescendo transition from forte into piano? What effect does a staccato articulation have on a tone? These are typical questions arising during analyzing and creating expressive music performances on the computer. We addressed these questions in a research project, performed detailed analyses of human performances and developed a series of mathematical models to emulate the characteristics that we observed. This chapter summarizes our analysis approach and compiles the mathematical models that we derived from the analyses. This comprizes a variety of macro and micro phenomena from the three domains timing, dynamics and articulation. A flexible model design makes it a versatile toolbox, esp. for music production, applicable to a variety of different musical styles.

## 4.1 Introduction

The expressive performance of music transforms a musical raw material (symbolic formats like music notation, MusicXML or MIDI) into a sounding output or an equivalent representation (i.e., audio data). A direct "one-to-one" mapping can be experienced by generating output directly from notated information where each note is precisely performed with its standardized pitch, duration, loudness, and timing. Though this may already be an expressive performance as it transforms the raw material into audio output, but in comparison to human musicians' performances this particular mapping appears to be a statistically insignificant special case.

A central aim of performance research in musicology as well as in the field of computer music is the identification and characterization of expressive performances. Another central aim is the investigation of typical applications in their application in specific musical contexts. The latter plays an intrinsic role for computer-generated performances. We denominate this *performance planning*, as it models the decision process that maps a musical situation to a combination of performance features, just like the musician who analyzes a musical piece. The musician then decides how he is going to play it, writes down an abstract performance plan by means of tempo, dynamics and articulation instructions. The rendering of a performance plan into an audible output or an equivalent representation is called *performance synthesis*. The goal of performance synthesis is to find formal models that adequately describe the performance phenomena. Typical questions are: How, precisely, is a ritardando played? What effect does a certain articulation have on a note? This is the toolkit for the work of performance planning.

This chapter is concerned with the latter field, performance synthesis, and summarizes respective results of an interdisciplinary research project of computer scientists and musicologists, who investigated the phenomena of expressive performance and developed mathematical models for their description. The technical implementation of these models has applications in music production, interactive media scoring, and interactive psychoacoustic studies. The models can also serve in performance analysis as they help abstracting from measurements (such as timing and loudness envelope measurements) and capturing meaningful features. Thereby we discovered, for instance, differences in the performance of continuous loudness transitions (crescendo, decrescendo) depending on the musical context. The following section gives an introduction to the performance features and their analysis—a comprehensive presentation is given by Hähnel (2013). Based on the findings, we detail and discuss the developed models, give remarks on their implementation and point out future directions of this research. Parts of this work have been previously presented by Berndt & Hähnel (2009, 2010), Hähnel & Berndt (2010), and Berndt (2011*a*,*b*).

## 4.2 Performance Features and Analyses

A musical score denotes a musical idea (or, which is more problematic, an idea of someone making a transcription). The performer analyzing the score derives a new musical idea, which can differ completely from the composer's

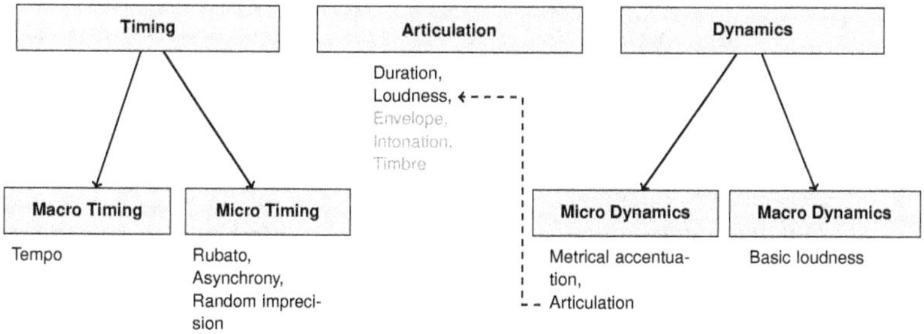


**Figure 4.1:** An overview of the performance feature classes described in this chapter. Envelope, intonation, and timbre are not included, thus, colored light gray.

idea. Expression in music performance aims at delivering the performer's idea of a musical score to the listener, who finally derives a new individual idea based on music perception and listening analysis. According to the modified lens model of Juslin (2009), music consists of acoustical cues, with which composer and performer want to achieve a certain kind of impression on the listener. The composer uses structural elements, like mode, pitch, melodic progression, and rhythm (which are in a strict sense rhythm classes, as Bengtsson (1974) wrote). The performer applies complex transformations, consciously and subconsciously. These transformations introduce a variety of details into the performance mainly with respect to the "three pillars" of expressive performance: timing, dynamics, and articulation. When developing models for phenomena in these domains it is not enough to know, e.g., that a ritardando slows down the tempo, that a crescendo raises the loudness, and that the time signature is somehow accentuated. We need to know precisely how these features are shaped. Which characteristics are appropriate and which degrees of freedom do they have? The succeeding section gives a brief introduction of the feature spaces discussed in this chapter, see Figure 4.1 for an overview. Following this, we detail our analysis methodology including the related work from which we then derive our modelling approach.

### 4.2.1 Feature Spaces

**Tempo** is the most deeply explored class of timing features. Tempo defines the musical meter in the format "number of symbolic time units per physical time unit", usually "beats per minute" (bpm). The tempo can remain constant. However, discrete and continuous tempo changes can be discovered over the course of a musical piece. Tempo changes are important means to work out climaxes, melodic target points, and musical form.

**Rubato** is differently defined in literature, Gatty (1912) counts four. The most widely used Riemannian definition describes rubati as short-term tempo fluctuation, the so-called "expressive timing"[1]. As this concept is already covered by tempo itself, we favor Hudson's (1994) definition of the "Early Baroque Rubato" as a timing distortion, that compensates within a certain time frame. This means that the stretching of some notes has to be compensated by a compression of the remaining notes within the same time frame and vice versa. Thus, the border between two frames is always synchronous with the underlying meter. The average tempo remains unchanged. Some definitions determine the time frame at the length of one measure. For the sake generality, we discard this constant henceforth and treat the length of the time frame as a variable parameter. These distortions may seem very subtle to the listener, but they are consciously performed "systematic variations" (Gabrielsson, Bengtsson & Gabrielsson 1983) trained by musicians (Quantz 1752, Hudson 1994), and are frequently applied to melodic figures, metrical stress points, melodic peaks, and used to set a certain rhythmic quality or "groove" (e.g., swing and Viennese waltz). In the latter case, the distortions are not only singular events but continuously recurrent.

**Constant asynchrony** introduces a temporal offset into the performance placing some musicians ahead and others behind. This often reflects the order and role of musical parts in the polyphonic setting (Rasch 1979). Leading parts are ahead while their accompaniment follows. A negative offset (being ahead) is a means to emphasize the respective notes. Besides its conscious application, asynchrony can also be an unintentional side effect of instrument playing specificities. Goebl (2001) explains the *Melody lead* phenomenon in pianist's performances in the context of motor conditions of piano playing, louder notes are struck faster, hence, are ahead.

**Random imprecision** affects the rhythmic accuracy of a musician's play. Human musicians are hardly able to reproduce a performance exactly (Yamada 1998, Madison 2000). Even if we consider biomechanical and instrument-related aspects such as fingering, bowing, key weight etc., there is a certain amount of variation that cannot yet be explained systematically.

[1] see also Goebl (2011), page 152.

Even though this may not be random, we chose this term in reference to the technical process that emulates it. Juslin, Friberg & Bresin (2002) state: "from an aesthetical point of view, random variations would seem to contribute to the 'living' character of music played by human beings. Thus, if we truly want to simulate human performance, we must incorporate this characteristic into the model."[2]

**Basic loudness** is the most prominent layer of dynamics. Like tempo, it comprizes constant loudness, discrete and continuous changes. The continuous changes (*crescendo, decrescendo*) are not only discretized in a note-by-note fashion but can also shape the individual loudness envelope of notes, the so-called *sub-note dynamics*. Basic loudness in general is of central importance to render phrase arcs, arcs of suspense, echo effects, express contrasts (hard/soft, relaxed/excited), to highlight a certain part in the polyphony, and to shape long notes (Bernhard 1667/1999).

**Metrical accentuation** sonifies the music's underlying time signature, rhythmic structure and implied stress points. It is a scheme of deviations from the basic loudness that is most commonly applied measure-wise. An example is the accentuation of each first beat in a measure. More complex accentuation schemes that reach over several measures can also be found (Berndt & Hähnel 2010). Metrical accentuation provides important cues that help the listener orientate in a stream of otherwise equally valued sound events and to abstract bigger structures. Without this dance is not thinkable.

**Articulation** determines the expressive character of each note (rhythmical, melodious, choppy, etc.) with regard to several dimensions. Nearly no note is performed as notated. Investigations were done by Bresin (2001) and Jerkert (2003) among others. Most performance systems refer to changes of *tone durations* as the primary articulation feature. But articulations that are primarily duration-related, like staccato and staccatissimo, often exert an influence also on the *loudness* (Hähnel & Berndt 2010). Many articulations primarily aim at the tones relative loudness (e.g., accent, sforzato, marcato). Beyond that, articulation also affects the tones' *loudness envelope, timbre,* and *intonation*. These latter three aspects will not be discussed here and remain future work in the context of this article. According to Riemann (1884) and Parncutt (2003) articulation and in particular the so-called *agogic accents* can also affect the timing of a performance (accentuation by anticipation or delay of the tone) which we will not discuss in

[2]Juslin et al. (2002), page 77.

this article either. Further research in articulation has been performed by Dannenberg, Pellerin & Derenyi (1998), Fyk (1995), and Maestre & Gómez (2005) among others.

### 4.2.2 Performance Analyses

In order to gain detailed insight into the characteristics and variety of performance features, we carried out a combination of *analysis-by-synthesis* (Gabrielsson 1985) and *analysis-by-measurement* approaches (de Poli 2004). From musicological literature and pedagogic treatises, for example Bernhard's (1667/1999) singing treatise and Quantz's (1752) treatise on flute playing, we get intuitive descriptions and clues about the effects of certain performance features. From these we know that articulation not only affects the duration of notes but their loudness as well, and that continuous loudness transitions (crescendo, decrescendo) should be shaped smoothly. Regarding micro timing Quantz (1752) invests much effort to specify an unequal playing of equally valued notes, an effect that today is called *inégalité*—chapter 5 provides a detailed introduction to this particular effect. Nonetheless, these intuitive descriptions are too vague for formal modelling.

More precise investigations and systematic measurements of human performances can be found in scientific literature in musicology, psychology and computer music. It is most notably the musical timing that was subject to a comprehensive research interest. Hefling (1993) and Hudson (1994) address inégalité, overdotting and further micro-timing aspects in great detail. Final ritardandi were analyzed by Sundberg & Verrillo (1980) and Honing (2003). The characteristics of ritardandi are related to the movement of stopping runners by Friberg & Sundberg (1999). Further timing research has been conducted by Todd (1995), Clarke (1999), and others. Also dynamics and articulation were subject to previous research by Dixon (2000), Jerkert (2003), Ramirez, Hazan & Maestre (2005), and Maestre & Gómez (2005) among others.

From these sources we derived initial model assumptions, tested them with professional and layman musicians during nine months of weekly rehearsal sessions and collected clues to which extent these basic characteristics could vary. On this basis we developed a series of preliminary models that describe the course of tempo and dynamics transitions, the shape of articulations and so on. Thanks to an extensive and partly optional parameterization, these models were very flexible, allowing a huge bandwidth of plausible and implausible characteristics, i.e. characteristics that we observed in human performances and those not observed so far. Based on detailed measurements in a variety of recordings we observed typical characteristics, revised and extended our models. Our study comprized 10 professional productions of G. P. Telemann's *Trumpet Concert in D major* (TWV 51:D7) from the repertoire of the library of the *Zentrum für Telemann-Pflege und -Forschung Magdeburg*[3], live recordings at the *5th International Telemann Competition for Historical Woodwinds* in 2009, and a series of specially devised exercises/etudes recorded with 10 professional musicians on historical and modern instruments (altogether 14 different instruments incl. strings, brass and woodwinds).

In these recordings we performed semiautomatic onset detection using the onset detection methods of Bello, Duxbury, Davies & Sandler (2004) and Dixon (2006) to generate a number of onset hypotheses. By tapping with the music we placed marks in this hypothesis space. Within a radius of 60–90 milliseconds around these marks we chose the highest peak in the onset detection function as the definite onset.

Tempo curves were derived from the inter-onset intervals and the underlying score representation. Knowing the onset of each tone, we can also do increasingly detailed loudness measurements. Here we have to distinguish between amplitude and timbre, the latter of which is very influential to the subjective loudness impression. The interaction between both is still subject to ongoing research. Hence, we measured only the sound pressure level. The music productions (the Telemann trumpet concertos), however, turned out to be inappropriate for loudness measurements, because of the scarcely documented, and thus mostly unknown, production process that introduces filtering and compression effects, manipulations in the mixing and other edits (Maempel 2011). Thus, for the dynamics and articulation measurements we only used the live and etude recordings, for which we had control over the acoustic circumstances allowing for good comparability. First, the loudness envelopes were extracted. The loudness of tones was measured at the end of the attack phase. Tone durations, more precisely tone offsets, were measured at the point where the magnitude of the envelope falls below 66 percent of the mean magnitude range of the articulation. Examples are shown in Figure 4.2.

The characteristics that we observed in the measurements were compared with those the models were able to create. The models were revised, adapted, and extended, accordingly. Wherever possible, their parameterization has been revised to provide more intuitive control over the features' details. The following sections document the state of the models after this process.

[3]engl.: Centre for Care and Research of Telemann's Music, Magdeburg.

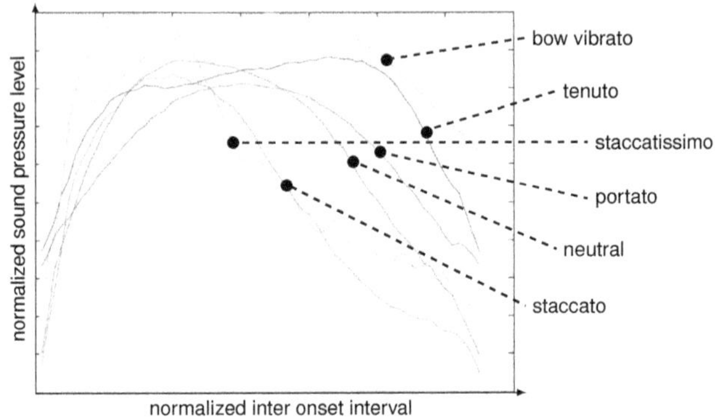


**Figure 4.2:** Mean envelopes for one performer playing a modern violin, analyzed and annotated with offset markers (•) by Hähnel (2013).

## 4.3 Timing

Timing in general is a mapping of symbolic time (e.g. score time and MIDI ticks) to physical time (typically in milliseconds). In addition to the well-known concept of tempo (here implemented by function $Ms$), further micro-timing transformations are incorporated: the rubato transformation ($Rubato$), a constant offset ($o_n$, in milliseconds), and a random deviation ($Rand(\sigma_j, \delta_j)$, in milliseconds). Each is detailed in the subsequent sections. All together form the timing conversion of symbolic date $d$ to milliseconds date $Timing(d)$.

$$Timing(d) = Ms(Rubato(d)) + o_n + Rand(\sigma_j, \delta_j)$$

The indices $n$ and $j$ need to be chosen appropriately, so that $d$ falls under the authority of the corresponding asynchrony and imprecision instructions.

### 4.3.1 Macro Timing / Tempo

Three kinds of tempo features can be distinguished: constant tempo, discrete tempo changes, and continuous tempo transitions. All of these are formally represented by tempo instructions $T$ that are organized in a sequential list, the so-called *tempo map* $M_T$.

$$M_T = (T_0, T_1, ..., T_n)$$

This formalism should be well known from modern sequencer software. The tempo map can also be interpreted as a sequence of curve segments that map symbolic time positions $d$ to tempo values $Tempo(d)$. This corresponds to the tempo events in the MIDI protocol. While these only define discrete tempo changes they are not able to describe continuous transition. Instead, a series of small tempo steps is used. Therefore, we extend this formalism and define a tempo instruction by the quintuple

$$T_m = (d_m,\ t_{1,m},\ t_{2,m},\ b_m,\ i_m) \quad \text{with} \quad m \in [0, n]$$

. The symbolic date of the instruction is indicated by $d_m$. We use MIDI ticks in the technical implementation as a symbolic time unit. The instruction defines a continuous tempo transition from $d_m$ to $d_{m+1}$, the latter is the date of the succeeding instruction or the end of the piece. The transition begins with tempo $t_{1,m}$ and ends with tempo $t_{2,m}$, both measured in bpm. The value of one beat is given by $b_m$ in floating-point format: e.g. quarter note $\rightarrow 0.25$, half note $\rightarrow 0.5$, and so on. This can easily be converted into MIDI ticks via the factor *PPQ* (pulses per quarter), which is part of each standard MIDI file header.

For constant tempo ($t_{1,m} = t_{2,m}$) this information already suffices. For continuous tempo transitions a further parameter is necessary for controlling the course of the transition over symbolic time, $i_m \in (0, 1)$. It indicates a relative position between $d_m$ and $d_{m+1}$ at which half of the tempo difference has to be processed.

$$Tempo((d_{m+1} - d_m)\, i_m + d_m) = 0.5\,(t_{1,m} + t_{2,m})$$

This *mean tempo condition* introduces an intuitive metaphor into timing control as it reflects the way musicians communicate this aspect (e.g. accelerate sooner; keep the bulk of change until the end, and so on). When $i_m = 0.5$ a linear transition is defined. The more $i_m$ differs from 0.5, the earlier ($i_m < 0.5$) or later ($0.5 < i_m$) is the mean tempo situated between $d_m$ and $d_{m+1}$, see also figure 4.3.

To determine the milliseconds date $Ms(d)$ of the symbolic date $d$, the integral of the inverse tempo function has to be computed. This is done segment-wise, where one segment corresponds to one tempo instruction.

$$Ms(d) = \begin{cases} d + Ms(0) & : \quad d \leq d_0 \\ \text{const}(d) + Ms(d_m) & : \quad t_{1,m} = t_{2,m} \\ \text{tran}(d) + Ms(d_m) & : \quad \text{otherwise} \end{cases}$$

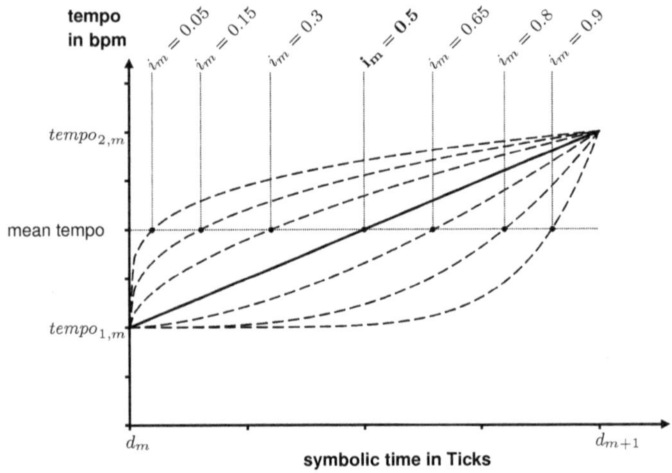


**Figure 4.3:** Tempo curves by power functions.

$Ms(0)$ is the playback start date, $d_0$ the date of the first instruction, and $m$ is the index of the latest instruction before $d$. Segments with constant tempo are processed by the function

$$\text{const}(d) = \frac{60\,000\,(d - d_m)}{t_{1,m}\,4\,b_m PPQ}$$

. Continuous tempo transitions are processed by the function tran. Here, the tempo curve is constructed using a power function in the unity square and scaled to the actual measurements of the instruction, as shown in figure 4.3. With this approach we deliberately decided not to follow the established phrase arch model (Repp 1992, Todd 1995) as this originates in the Romantic performance tradition and is hardly generalizable and applicable to other performance styles, e.g. from the Baroque period. Furthermore, it mixes performance modelling issues and aesthetic decisions on the level of the performance planning, in particular musical phrasing, which we wanted to keep apart. However, Friberg, Bresin & Sundberg's (2006) implementation of the phrase arch model within the KTH rule system composes the arcs from power functions with variable exponents and did, insofar, already demonstrate the applicability of power functions for tempo transitions as we do it here, too (Friberg 1995).

$$Tempo(d) = \left(\frac{d - d_m}{d_{m+1} - d_m}\right)^{\mathrm{p}(i_m)} (t_{2,m} - t_{1,m}) + t_{1,m}$$

The exponent $\mathrm{p}(i_m) = (\ln 0.5)/(\ln i_m)$ implements the *mean tempo condition*. The milliseconds date $\mathrm{tran}(d)$ can now be approximated by $\widetilde{\mathrm{tran}}(d)$ via numerical integration of the inverse tempo function (using Simpson's rule with $N/2$ iterations and even $N$).

$$\begin{aligned}\widetilde{\mathrm{tran}}(d) \quad &= \quad \frac{d - d_m}{3N}\left(\frac{1}{Tempo(x_0)} + \sum_{k=1}^{\frac{N}{2}-1} \frac{2}{Tempo(x_{2k})}\right. \\ &\qquad \left. + \sum_{k=1}^{N/2} \frac{4}{Tempo(x_{2k-1})} + \frac{1}{Tempo(x_N)}\right) \frac{60\,000}{4b_m PPQ} \\ &\qquad \text{with} \quad x_k = d_m + k\frac{d - d_m}{N}\end{aligned}$$

The approximation accuracy can be controlled by $N$. But how much accuracy is necessary? Big $N$ may be desirable in the context of certain applications beyond the mere "music for listening", for instance, for some synchrony reasons. The application is, of course, free to choose any setting. But the computation time increases together with $N$. Hence, too high a setting might be avoided in the context of realtime applications, like interactive and adaptive music.

We have also experimented with an implicit approach (Berndt 2011*a*). Here the tempo curves are not modelled explicitly. Instead, we bypass the modelling of the tempo curve and the integration step by constructing the timing curve directly, based on rational quadratic Bézier curves. These are constructed in a way that the mean tempo condition holds. Considering the effort for construction and re-parameterization the implicit approach did bring no considerable gain of computing performance, though.

The resulting shapes of the corresponding tempo curves of the implicit approach are similar but not identical to the explicit approach. This, together with the integration accuracy issue of the explicit approach, raised the following question: To which extent are human listeners able to distinguish different tempo curves? We conducted a listener study with 18 participants (7 musicians and 11 non-musicians). As stimuli we rendered 6 pairs of tempo transitions on the same musical material. The participants were asked to decide whether these were different or identical (indistinguishable). For better orientation we also provided the sheet

| | $i_m$ settings | | | correct answers | | |
|---|---|---|---|---|---|---|
| type | 1st | 2nd | diff. | # | % | significance |
| acccel. | 0.7 | 0.3 | 0.4 | 16 | 88.9 | **0.001** |
| rit. | 0.5 | 0.4 | 0.1 | 5 | 27.8 | 0.096 |
| acccel. | 0.6 | 0.8 | 0.2 | 9 | 50.0 | 1.0 |
| rit. | 0.4 | 0.4 | 0 | 8 | 44.4 | 0.815 |
| acccel. | 0.4 | 0.3 | 0.1 | 9 | 50.0 | 1.0 |
| rit. | 0.3 | 0.6 | 0.3 | 14 | 77.8 | **0.031** |

**Table 4.1:** The results of the listener study with 18 participants. Six pairs of continuous tempo transitions had to be classified as identical or different. They differed only with respect to the parameter $i_m$.

music of the stimuli. The tempo transitions were all of the same length, 16 measures with $4/4$ time signature. All accelerandi began with 40 bpm and ended up with 120 bpm. All ritardandi began with 120 bpm and decelerated to 40 bpm. Only the parameter $i_m$, that controls the course of the tempo curve, was different. The music was rendered with the explicit model at $N = 512$ (that is a segmentation for each 16th note).

The outcome of the study is given in table 4.1. The participants were clearly able to recognize contrary curve characteristics, that is, "root shape" ($i_m < 0.5$) against "potential shape" ($i_m > 0.5$), which can be found in the first and sixth pair of tempo transitions. All other pairs with differing $i_m$ up to 0.2 could not be distinguished significantly. In our music examples the 0.2 difference produced tempo differences of 10 up to 23 bpm lasting for 10 measures. The resulting timing difference was 15 seconds. Even the 0.1 difference caused tempo differences of 5 up to 8 bpm over 10 measures and timing differences of still 4 seconds. Based on this, we can span a narrowband around an ideal tempo curve and its corresponding timing curve by varying the parameter $i_m \pm 0.1$. As long as the approximation is staying within this narrowband the difference seems negligible to the average listener, as the results indicate. Specifically, this means that relatively rough and fast approximations with $N \in \{2, 4\}$ are already sufficient for most purposes.

### 4.3.2 Rubato

Rubato is a timing distortion that compensates within a certain frame of symbolic time. It can occur as a singular feature (e.g. stretching of a melodic peak)

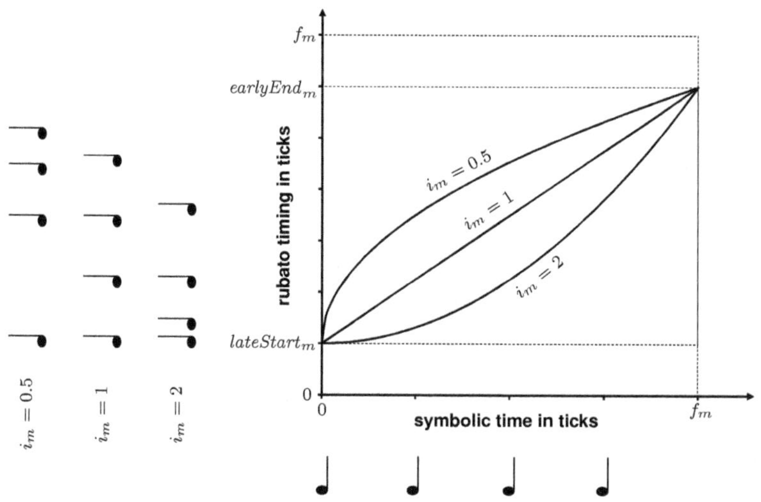


**Figure 4.4:** Three rubato schemes that differ in parameter $i_m$. The frame length $f_m$ is 4/4.

or as a recurrent scheme (e.g. swing timing and Viennese waltz). The characteristic of the distortion is not static but can be altered over the course of a piece. Therefore, all rubato instructions $R$ are arranged in a sequential list, the *rubato map*.

$$M_R = (R_0, R_1, ..., R_r)$$

. One such instruction $R$ defines a timing distortion scheme as illustrated in figure 4.4.

$$R_m = (d_m, f_m, i_m, lateStart_m, earlyEnd_m) \quad \text{for} \quad m \in [0, r]$$

The scheme is repeatedly applied frame by frame starting at symbolic date $d_m$. The frame length is $f_m$. This means that all dates $d_m + kf_m$ with $k \in \mathbb{N}_0$ fall together with the undistorted macro timing. The distortion is modeled via the power function $x^{i_m}$ in the interval $[0, 1]$ and then scaled to $[0, f_m]$. The exponent controls the shape of the distortion, i.e. stretching followed by compression or vice versa. The two variables $lateStart_m$ and $earlyEnd_m$ introduce a further optional scaling without changing the frame length. To ensure the sequential order of musical events, the relation $0 \leq lateStart_m < earlyEnd_m \leq 1$ must hold. The rubato distortion of symbolic timing is computed as follows.

$$\begin{aligned} Rubato(d) &= \text{frameDate}(d) \\ &+ \left[ \left( \frac{(d - d_m) \bmod f_m}{f_m} \right)^{i_m} (earlyEnd_m - lateStart_m) + lateStart_m \right] f_m \end{aligned}$$

$$\text{where} \quad \text{frameDate}(d) = d - [(d - d_m) \bmod f_m] \quad \text{and} \quad d \in (d_m, d_{m+1}]$$

### 4.3.3 Constant Asynchrony

Asynchrony in ensemble play is a temporal offset of some parts. It often reflects their role in the polyphony (lead, accompaniment, bass, etc.). This role may change during the piece. So does its temporal offset. Hence, we formalize asynchrony instructions $S$ arranged in an *asynchrony map*

$$M_S = (S_0, S_1, ..., S_s)$$

for a certain part. One such instruction has the form

$$S_n = (d_n, o_n)$$

. The attribute $d_n$ denotes the symbolic date from when on the offset $o_n$ (in milliseconds) is applied to all succeeding events until $d_{n+1}$ or the end of the piece.

### 4.3.4 Random Imprecision

Random imprecision is a concession to the fact that not all timing details in human performances can be explained systematically. These deviations are modelled using a Gaussian distribution with standard deviation $\sigma$ (in milliseconds) and expected value $0$. In order to exclude extreme and implausible outliers we further clip the values at a maximum deviation $\pm\delta$ (in milliseconds). An *imprecision map*

$$M_I = (I_0, I_1, ..., I_i)$$

arranges all imprecision instructions

$$I_j = (d_j, \sigma_j, \delta_j) \quad \text{with} \quad j \in [0, i]$$

in temporal order. From symbolic date $d_j$ all note onsets are subject to the random imprecision defined by $I_j$ and computed by function $Rand(\sigma_j, \delta_j)$.

Such randomness can also be found in dynamics and articulation data. Modern samplers partly support this via alternative samples—playing the same note again triggers a different sample. Introducing a similar kind of functionality to the succeeding dynamics and articulation models is straight forward and not further detailed in this text.

## 4.4 Dynamics

The concept of macro and micro features in dynamics is similar to that of timing. Macro dynamics defines a basic loudness curve while micro dynamics add deviations to the curve. As articulation also affects the loudness, it is a micro dynamics feature, too. However, articulation also affects a series of other attributes as well, and is traditionally discussed separately. We follow this convention and discuss articulation in a separate section.

The loudness of a tone is not sufficiently defined by its amplitude. Equally important is its timbre. Loud tones *sound* loud. The attack phase of a tone's amplitude envelope influences its loudness perception, too. Fortunately, these aspects are covered by most modern synthesizers and samplers and are mapped to a single parameter. The MIDI standard calls this parameter "velocity". The models described in the subsequent sections build upon this. What is computed in the following is the velocity value of each note.

### 4.4.1 Macro Dynamics / Basic Loudness

Although dynamics have been notated in musical scores for several centuries, typical dynamics instructions like *pp*, *mp*, and *f* are still ambiguous. How loud is forte? The answer differs from piece to piece, instrument to instrument, and even from sound generator to sound generator (Dannenberg 2006). To address this issue, we put a header $H$ at the beginning of each *dynamics map* $M_D$.

$$M_D = (H, (D_0, D_1, ..., D_n))$$

It defines a lookup table that assigns velocity values to character strings, both freely definable. An example is shown in Table 4.2. In a polyphonic setting every musical part can have its own dynamics map. Their headers can define

| String | *ppp* | *pp* | *p* | *mp* | *mf* | *f* | *ff* | *fff* |
|---|---|---|---|---|---|---|---|---|
| MIDI Velocity | 12 | 36 | 48 | 64 | 83 | 97 | 111 | 125 |

**Table 4.2:** An example lookup table that assigns MIDI velocity values to character strings. As the header of each dynamics map, it defines the vocabulary of dynamics instructions.

different values. Forte in the flute can differ from forte in the trumpet. After the header $H$ follows the sequence of dynamics instructions.

$$D = (d_m, v_{1,m}, v_{2,m}, \text{shape}_m) \quad \text{with} \quad m \in [0, n]$$

An instruction defines the date $d_m$ from when the basic loudness $v_{1,m}$ transitions to $v_{2,m}$ until $d_{m+1}$ or the end of the piece. This corresponds to the typical crescendo and decrescendo notation ($mp < mf$). Both, $v_{1,m}$ and $v_{2,m}$, are either numeric velocity values or character strings from the header.

For a constant basic loudness both $v$-values are set equal. Otherwise, they define a substantial (de-)crescendo. For these transitions, our measurements have shown various sigmoidal characteristics which we construct from cubic Bézier curves within the unity square and then scale to the actual measurements of the transition. The control polygon is spanned by the four points

$$P_0 = (0,0), \quad P_1 = (x_1, 0), \quad P_2 = (x_2, 1), \quad \text{and} \quad P_3 = (1,1)$$

of which only the horizontal positions of $P_1$ and $P_2$ are responsible for a particular shaping (see figure 4.5). This simplifies the $y$-component of the curve's polynomials.

$$\begin{aligned} x(t) &= (3x_1 - 3x_2 + 1)t^3 + (-6x_1 + 3x_2)t^2 + 3x_1 t \\ y(t) &= -2t^3 + 3t^2 \end{aligned}$$

The loudness of an event at date $d \in [d_m, d_{m+1})$ is then computed by function $MacroDyn$.

$$MacroDyn(d) = y(t_d) \cdot (v_{2,m} - v_{1,m}) + v_{1,m} \quad \text{for} \quad x(t_d) = \frac{d - d_m}{d_{m+1} - d_m}$$

However, as $x_1$ and $x_2$ are non-intuitive parameters, we introduce two rather intuitive ones. *Curvature* $c_m \in [0, 1]$ controls the "intensity" of the S-shape and *protraction* $p_m \in [-1, 1]$ distorts the symmetry of the curve. They are specified by the term

$$\text{shape}_m = (c_m, p_m, res_m)$$

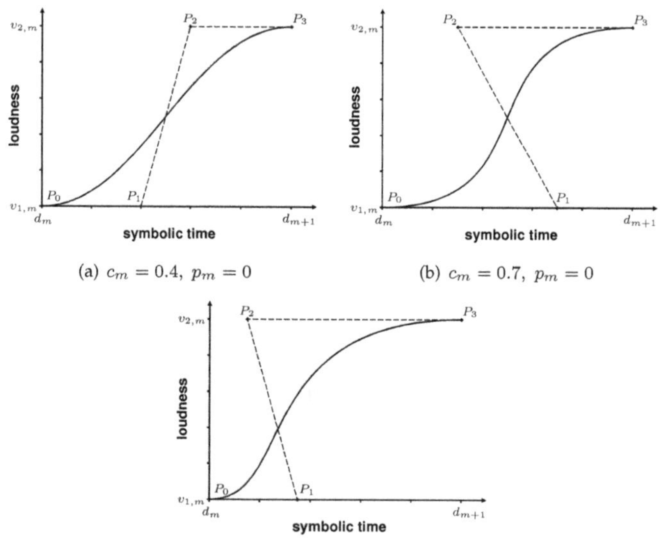


(a) $c_m = 0.4,\ p_m = 0$

(b) $c_m = 0.7,\ p_m = 0$

(c) $c_m = 0.7,\ p_m = -0.5$

**Figure 4.5:** De-/Crescendi are modelled by cubic Bézier curves. Control point $P_2$ and $P_3$ determine its characteristic. The parameters for this are *curvature* $c_m$ and *protraction* $p_m$.

and map onto $x_1$ and $x_2$ in the following way.

$$x_1 = \frac{p_m + |p_m|}{2} + c_m(1 - |p_m|)\ , \quad x_2 = \frac{p_m - |p_m|}{2} - c_m(1 - |p_m|) + 1$$

The third parameter $res_m \in (0, 1]$ sets the temporal resolution when the transition is rendered not in a note-by-note fashion, but into controller movement (e.g. the channel volume slider). A value of 0.1, for instance, subdivides the transition into 10 controller steps, 0.01 into 100, and so on.

To identify typical settings of both parameters, curvature and protraction, we analyzed human performed crescendi and decrescendi. The 10 musicians, who participated in our study (see section 4.2.2), had to perform crescendi and decrescendi in unmusical etudes (in fact, tone repetitions) as well as in musical melodies. After approximation and plotting into the curvature-protraction domain we observed a striking difference. The etude transitions mostly clustered around $(0, 0)$, which creates a very neutral, nearly linear shape, whereas in

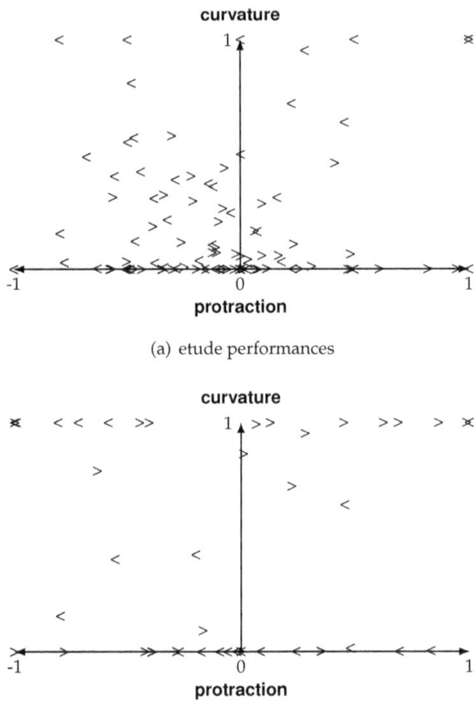


(a) etude performances

(b) musical performances

**Figure 4.6:** Observed combinations of curvature and protraction for crescendi (<) and decrescendi (>) in our performance measurements.

a more musical context we observed mostly extreme curvature values ($c_m \in \{0, 1\}$) and a higher variance of protraction (see figure 4.6). A detailed description and discussion of the study can be found at Hähnel (2013).

### 4.4.2 Metrical Accentuation

Metrical and rhythmical structure often suggest specific accentuation schemes that recur measure-wise. They render the distinction between "weak" beats and "strong" beats, the perceptual grouping of pulses according to a metrical and rhythmical structure. Such an accentuation scheme defines the contour of deviations from the underlying macro dynamics.

Metrical accentuation overlays with other dynamics features and room acoustics. This makes it extremely difficult to get clear empirical measurements from music recordings. We could make some observations in the performance exercises (see section 4.2.2), but these do not allow generalization, yet. Therefore, the metrical accentuation model, that is described in the following, mainly derives from descriptions in theoretical and pedagogic sources, like instrumental lesson books and interviews with professional music teachers. Its validation through measurements, for instance regarding the shape of transitions between accents, still remains an open question.

Formally, we embed the metrical accentuation scheme in an emphasis instruction $E$. All emphasis instructions are organized in an *emphasis map* $M_E$.

$$M_E = (E_0, E_1, ..., E_n)$$

One instruction has the form

$$E_m = \left(d_m, scale_m, \left(A_m^0, A_m^1, ..., A_m^k\right)\right) \quad \text{with} \quad m \in [0, n]$$

. From symbolic date $d_m$ the emphasis instruction is applied to all succeeding measures up to $d_{m+1}$ or the end of the piece. It further defines a sequence of accentuations $A_m^{0...k}$, the actual accentuation scheme.

An accentuation

$$A_m^j = (beat_{j,m}, a_{1,j,m}, a_{2,j,m}, a_{3,j,m}) \text{ with } j \in [0, k], a_{i,j,m} \in [-1, 1], \ i \in \{1, 2, 3\}$$

represents one segment of the scheme. The segment begins with beat $beat_{j,m}$ (for the first beat in the measure $beat_{j,m} = 1$, second beat $beat_{j,m} = 2$ etc.) and ends with $beat_{j,m+1}$ or the end of the measure. Hence, in a 3/4-time signature any accentuation with $beat_{j,m} \geq 4$ will be ignored since the next bar already begins at the fourth beat. Generally, $beat_{j,m}$ is a floating-point value, so that an emphasis can be defined at any position within the bar. A value of $beat_{j,m} = 2.5$ designates beat "two-and". The accentuation at position $beat_{j,m}$ is set by $a_{1,j,m}$. A value of 1 sets the strongest accentuation; 0 causes no deviation from the basic loudness; $-1$ indicates maximal restraint. These values are scaled by attribute $scale_m$ to actual loudness values and then added onto the macro dynamics. However, if that value exceeds the numerical range (0 to 127 in MIDI), $scale_m$ is automatically decreased in our implementation. This ensures a differentiated accentuation as far as possible. This behavior, furthermore, matches an equivalence that can be observed with human musicians: accentuation is less pronounced at the borders of the dynamic range.

To describe what happens in-between two accentuations a linear transition is introduced which ranges from $a_{2,j,m}$ to $a_{3,j,m}$. Both parameters are optional. Without them, a constant emphasis of $a_{1,j,m}$ is set on the whole segment. If the notes in-between the accentuated positions shall be set at a different level, $a_{2,j,m}$ is used. This alone produces a constant emphasis that might suffice for most situations in musical practice.

The accentuated loudness (MIDI velocity, respectively) of an event on date $d$ is computed by function $EmphDyn$. The beat position of $d$ within the measure (in floating-point format) is encoded as $\mathrm{beat}(d)$.

$$EmphDyn(d) = MacroDyn(d) + \mathrm{accent}(d) \cdot \mathrm{scale}(d)$$

$$\mathrm{accent}(d) = \begin{cases} a_{1,j,m} : \mathrm{beat}(d) = beat_{j,m} \\ \dfrac{(\mathrm{beat}(d) - beat_{j,m})(a_{3,j,m} - a_{2,j,m})}{beat_{j+1,m} - beat_{j,m}} + a_{2,j,m} : \mathrm{otherwise} \end{cases}$$

$$\mathrm{scale}(d) = \begin{cases} MacroDyn(d) : MacroDyn(d) + \mathrm{accent}(d) \cdot scale_m < 0 \\ 127 - MacroDyn(d) : MacroDyn(d) + \mathrm{accent}(d) \cdot scale_m > 127 \\ scale_m : \mathrm{otherwise} \end{cases}$$

$$\text{where} \quad d_m \leq d < d_{m+1} \quad \text{and} \quad beat_{j,m} \leq \mathrm{beat}(d) < beat_{j+1,m}$$

## 4.5 Articulation

Identical articulation instructions are rendered differently in different musical contexts. An articulation can even be inhomogeneous within a single musical piece and style. A standard articulation in a light-footed Baroque dance is shorter and more detached than in Romantic hymns. The articulation vocabulary has expanded and changed throughout music history. Some basic articulations were established in the Baroque era. The Romantic period and Serialism invented further articulations and finer differentiations of the Baroque articulations. Moreover, multiple articulation instructions can be combined. E.g. an accent can be added to any articulation to signal additional dynamic emphasis. Our model provides a flexible customizability.

This lead us to the basic concept of formally separate definitions of articulations and their application to a specific musical context. Therefore, we introduce the formalisms *articulation style* and *articulation map*. An articulation style is a pool of articulation definitions. One such definition describes the manipulations which the articulation makes to an input note. This definition can be freely edited to create any articulations. Several styles with possibly differing definitions can be defined. An articulation map is a sequence of instructions to articulate a specific musical context. Only high-level descriptors are used which act as lookup references to the definitions in an articulation style.

### 4.5.1 Articulation Style

An articulation style $AStyle$ is an element of a set of styles

$$AStyleSet = \{AStyle_0, AStyle_1, ..., AStyle_t\}$$

and defines a set of articulation instructions.

$$AStyle_s = \{A_0^s, A_1^s, ..., A_b^s\} \quad \text{for} \quad 0 \leq s \leq t$$

An articulation instruction defines the manipulations it applies to an input note by a list of manipulators $M$.

$$A_a^s = (M_0^{s,a}, M_1^{s,a}, ..., M_n^{s,a}) \quad \text{for} \quad 0 \leq a \leq b$$

One such manipulator is a triple which indicates the mode and value of the manipulation, and the note attribute to be changed.

$$M_m^{s,a} = (mode_m^{s,a}, attribute_m^{s,a}, value_m^{s,a}) \quad \text{for} \quad 0 \leq m \leq n$$

Three modes of manipulation are defined. These either set absolute values or cause relative value changes ($note$ is the input note, $Attribute(note)$ denotes the note attribute to be edited).

$$Attribute(note) := \begin{cases} value_m^{s,a} & : \text{ set mode} \\ Attribute(note) + value_m^{s,a} & : \text{ add mode} \\ Attribute(note) \cdot value_m^{s,a} & : \text{ percental mode} \end{cases}$$

Possible attributes are the note's velocity ("$velocity$"), its duration in the symbolic time domain ("$tickDur$"), and its duration in the physical time domain ("$msDur$").

$$Attribute(note) = \begin{cases} Velocity(note) & : \ attribute_m^{s,a} = \text{“}velocity\text{”} \\ symbDuration(note) & : \ attribute_m^{s,a} = \text{“}tickDur\text{”} \\ msDuration(note) & : \ attribute_m^{s,a} = \text{“}msDur\text{”} \end{cases}$$

| string identifier of articulation | modifiers | | |
|---|---|---|---|
| | *mode* | *attribute* | *value* |
| Accent | add | velocity | 25 |
| Sforzato | set | velocity | 127 |
| Cesura | add | msDur | -400 |
| Pizzicato | set | msDur | 1 |
| Spiccato | set | msDur | 160 |
| | add | velocity | 25 |
| Staccatissimo | set | msDur | 160 |
| | add | velocity | 5 |
| Staccato | set | msDur | 180 |
| | add | velocity | -5 |
| Portato | percental | tickDur | 0.8 |
| Marcato | percental | tickDur | 0.8 |
| | add | velocity | 25 |
| Tenuto | percental | tickDur | 0.9 |
| | add | velocity | 12 |
| Nonlegato | percental | tickDur | 0.95 |
| Legato | percental | tickDur | 1 |

**Table 4.3:** The settings of the manipulators for some typical articulations.

Absolute millisecond durations and changes are of particular importance for short articulations such as *staccato* and for caesuras (breathing pauses), as these tend to have a static length independent of the underlying timing. In the implementation, the style index $s$ and the instruction index $a$ are replaced by unique name strings. These descriptors are further used to trigger specific samples and loudness envelopes in the sound generator to benefit from prefabricated high-quality material for *staccato*, *portato*, *legato*, etc. Moreover, the developer of an articulation style is free to define and name any articulation. Only the "standard" articulation plays a special role as it is applied to all notes except for those with individual instructions in the articulation map. Some typical examples are shown in Table 4.3.

### 4.5.2 Articulation Map

The articulation map $M_A$ is a sequentially ordered list with two types of elements, *style switches* and *articulators*. A style switch is a triple

$$switch = (d, s, a_{standard}) \text{ where } AStyle_s \in AStyleSet \text{ and } A^s_{a_{standard}} \in AStyle_s$$

. The style switch designates the articulation style $AStyle_s$ as lookup style from date $d$ on until the next switch and sets a standard articulation $a_{standard}$, which applies to any note that is not articulated otherwise. The first element in an articulation map has to be a style switch. The other elements in the map are articulators, having the form

$$articulator = (note, (a_0, a_1, ..., a_k)) \quad \text{with} \quad A^s_{a_{0...k}} \in AStyle_s$$

. Articulators indicate the *note* to be articulated and the articulation instructions $a_{0...k}$. The instructions are successively applied to the note. Combinations of several instructions are possible, like an accentuated legato

$$(note, (\text{“}Legato\text{”}, \text{“}Accent\text{”}))$$

or a double accent

$$(note, (\text{“}Accent\text{”}, \text{“}Accent\text{”}))$$

. In the latter case, one accent may raise the velocity by a certain amount, double accent does it twice then.

## 4.6 Some Remarks on Implementation

All models were implemented in a MIDI-based performance rendering engine, that takes a raw MIDI file and a higher-level description of its expressive performance in XML format as input. The XML file can contain several different performances of the same musical piece.

Each map (tempo map, dynamics map, emphasis map, etc.) can be defined globally for all parts in the polyphonic setting or locally for just one part. Global maps are used to define overall features, e.g. a global tempo map for all parts as they play synchronously. Local maps introduce features that are rendered by only one part. For instance, micro timing deviations coinciding with melodic figures that occur only in particular parts. If both, a global and a local map are available for a part, the local map overrules the global map. This allows us to create highly polyphonic performance structures. A typical situation in a solo concert would be modelled as follows. Global maps are defined for the accompaniment, whereas, for the solo instrument which has its own more detailed musical structure demanding a more detailed performance, local maps are created.

Our performance engine further implements techniques to transition seamlessly between different performances. This allows us to combine them and create new performances interactively during realtime playback and opens up for live situations, like interactive media scoring (Berndt 2009, Berndt, Dachselt & Groh 2012), music-psychological studies involving a certain amount of interactivity, and analysis-by-synthesis studies (see chapter 5 for an example).

## 4.7 General Discussion & Future Directions

During the development of the models, we paid particular attention to make them easy to customize and easy to combine. The models support a big variety of characteristics covering those observed in the measurements of human musicians as well as atypical and extreme degeneracies, e.g. very strong micro timing distortions that hardly occur in human performances. Most models allow the definition of new instances, like accentuation schemes, dynamics instructions, and articulations. This flexibility opens up the whole bandwidth of performance styles for music production and pays off in study applications, especially when the study should not only cover typical characteristics.

In order to properly combine different models it is mandatory to prevent mutual interference. A micro timing distortion (rubato) affects local tempo fluctuations, but the average tempo remains unchanged. The same applies to metrical accentuation, articulation, and basic loudness. An articulation may change the loudness of a note, but the basic loudness and metrical accentuation are preserved. Our model design enables a change of one feature without affecting the other feature, even if they are interweaving on the same domain.

For the evaluation of which extent our models are able to describe plausible human performances (in Western music culture), we carried out a listener study with 46 participants. 23 of them had an expert background in historically informed music performance. The study consisted of two runs. In the first run, the listeners had to decide whether the musical samples they heard were real (human) or synthetic (computer) performances and grade it (1: human performance, 2: probably human, 3: probably synthetic, 4: synthetic). In the second run, all samples were synthetic performances and the listeners had to decide whether these were copies of human performances (1: yes, 2: probably yes, 3: probably no, 4: no).

All samples were Baroque pieces, mostly minuets. The 1:1 copies were detailed manual reproductions of real performances that correspond with them regarding timing (similar inter-onset intervals), dynamics, and articulation (transcribed from close-listening analyses and readjusted with respect to the used instrumental sample set). The plausible versions were replications of these performances using our models without random imprecision. The articulation-only performances excluded the work with timing and dynamics features, and kept only the constant asynchrony and articulations of the plausible versions. The extreme versions use the same characteristics as the plausible versions, but set extreme shapes (exaggerated rubati and articulations etc.). In the inverted versions the tempo, macro dynamics, rubato, and metrical accentuation characteristics are inverse to the 1:1 copies. Both, the extreme and inverted versions were untypical performances serving as control stimuli.

All versions worked with high-quality samples from the *Vienna Symphonic Library* (Vienna Symphonic Library GmbH 2015) and applied reverberation and stereo panning based on the human recordings. As the differences in sound generation and acoustics, nonetheless, most likely biased the results of the first part of the study, we excluded the human recordings in the second part. The 1:1 copies served as reference performances.

Table 4.4 shows a summary of the listener's ratings. A significance analysis of the rating differences reveals that, in the first test, the human recordings were rated significantly better than all other versions by both, expert and non-expert listeners. The mean rankings of the plausible (model-based) versions and the articulation-only versions were not significantly different from the 1:1 copies indicating that an elaborate articulation strongly contributes to the impression of plausibility. Significantly different ratings occurred between the plausible versions and the control group of extreme and inverse versions in both tests—the control groups were rated significantly worse. The models prove to lie in level with the reference versions. This suggests that the models are able to plausibly emulate typical characteristics of human performances.

The surprisingly good ratings of the articulation-only versions also have to be seen in the stylistic context of our stimuli, i.e. all Baroque music. Flat macro features and an intense work with micro features is close to the performance concepts of music of this style, confers the study of Shaffer (1981). With music

| Type of performance | 23 non-expert ratings | | 23 expert ratings | |
|---|---|---|---|---|
| | mean value | standard dev. | mean value | standard dev. |
| | " The current recording is real." | | | |
| human recordings | 1.70 | 0.470 | 1.35 | 0.487 |
| 1:1 copies | 2.61 | 0.656 | 3.65 | 0.573 |
| plausible models | 2.52 | 0.665 | 3.35 | 0.775 |
| inverted & extreme versions | 2.35 | 0.775 | 3.26 | 0.915 |
| | "This synthetic version is a copy of a real performance." | | | |
| 1:1 copies | 2.22 | 0.751 | 2.44 | 0.609 |
| inverted versions | 2.76 | 0.705 | 2.96 | 0.767 |
| plausible models | 2.26 | 0.619 | 2.48 | 0.846 |
| extreme versions | 2.94 | 0.460 | 3.11 | 0.656 |
| articulation only | 2.22 | 0.736 | 1.87 | 0.757 |

**Table 4.4:** Listeners' ratings in the study.

from the Romantic period, we would expect to gain a rather significant difference to the 1:1 copies.

The models may already cover a big variety of performance features, but in the measurements we still observe a lot of details that cannot be captured yet. Random processes might be used to emulate what cannot even be derived from systematic reasons. There are also a lot of performance aspects not covered yet, such as fingering and bowing (Al Kasimi, Nichols & Raphael 2007, Hall & O'Donnell 2009), or the communication within ensemble play. The interaction between the players functions like a homeostatic system. Little timing variances of one player affect neighboring players, who gradually adapt to it. The player himself also tries to restore synchrony with the ensemble. Similar effects exist for dynamics and articulation. Their investigation and formalization still stands out and would be a valuable extension.

Although our models introduce a certain level of abstraction and offer a fairly intuitive parameterization, the creation of expressive performances is, nonetheless, a laborious process. The models constitute a comprehensive toolbox. However, the creation of a performance plan is still up to the user. This work can be supported by algorithmic methods, not necessarily like a fully autonomous virtual musician, but as music production tools which create initial performances that can be refined by human musicians. Building such a framework around the models described here is a promising future perspective of this work.

## 4.8 Summary

The expressive performance of music is not a simple one-to-one transformation of notated information into sounding output. Forms of printed music are known to be ambiguous and incomplete, which gives freedom to musicians when designing their own interpretations. However, studies have shown that musical culture has established certain design patterns. We traced the establishment of these patterns in musicological and theoretical literature (mainly on Western music), and found clues about their characteristics. This was complemented by analyses of audio recordings, including professional CD productions, life recordings at an international competition, and carefully prepared exercises. We gained valuable insights, not only into the basic characteristics and shapes of the phenomena, but also into their mutability. Based on these insights, we were able to develop a series of dedicated mathematical models. We see these models as a versatile and flexible toolkit for the creation of expressive performances with—

but not limited to—human-like impression. Potential applications can be found in music production, expressive performance generation, realtime adaptive music performance, analysis-by-synthesis studies, and as a musicological tool to emulate historically informed performance practices.

**Acknowledgement** The author would like to express thanks to all musicians who participated in the recordings, to all participants of the studies, to the team of the "Zentrum für Telemann-Pflege und -Forschung Magdeburg", in particular Carsten Lange, for the cooperation, inspiring discussions, and the chance to make recordings at the *5th International Telemann Competition for Historical Woodwinds* in 2009. My sincere thanks are also dedicated to Tilo Hähnel who cooperated with me in this project, conducted the studies and analyses, and, thereby, provided the invaluable basis for the iterative revision process in the model development.

## Bibliography

Al Kasimi, A., Nichols, E. & Raphael, C. (2007), A Simple Algorithm for Automatic Generation of Polyphonic Piano Fingerings, *in* '10th Int. Society for Music Information Retrieval Conf. (ISMIR)', Austrian Computer Society (OCG), Vienna Univerity of Technology, Vienna, Austria, pp. 131–132.

Bello, J., Duxbury, C., Davies, M. & Sandler, M. (2004), 'On the Use of Phase and Energy for Musical Onset Detection in the Complex Domain', *IEEE Signal Processing Letters* **11**(6), 553–556.

Bengtsson, I. (1974), Empirische Rhythmusforschung in Uppsala, *in* 'Hamburger Jahrbuch für Musikwissenschaft', Lang, Frankfurt a.M., pp. 195–220.

Berndt, A. (2009), Musical Nonlinearity in Interactive Narrative Environments, *in* G. Scavone, V. Verfaille & A. da Silva, eds, 'Proc. of the Int. Computer Music Conf. (ICMC)', International Computer Music Association, Schulich School of Music/McGill University, Montreal, Canada, pp. 355–358.

Berndt, A. (2011*a*), Musical Tempo Curves, *in* M. Clarke, M. Adkins & B. Isaacs, eds, 'Proc. of the Int. Computer Music Conf. (ICMC)', International Computer Music Association, University of Huddersfield, Huddersfield, UK, pp. 118–121.

Berndt, A. (2011*b*), *Musik für interaktive Medien: Arrangement- und Interpretationstechniken*, Verlag Dr. Hut, Munich, Germany.

Berndt, A., Dachselt, R. & Groh, R. (2012), A Survey of Variation Techniques for Repetitive Games Music, *in* 'Audio Mostly 2012: 6th Conf. on Interaction with Sound—Sound and Future Vision', Ionian Academy, Interactive Institute/Sonic Studio Piteå, ACM SIGCHI, Corfu, Greece, pp. 61–67.

Berndt, A. & Hähnel, T. (2009), Expressive Musical Timing, *in* 'Audio Mostly 2009: 4th Conf. on Interaction with Sound—Sound and Emotion', Glasgow Caledonian University, Interactive Institute/Sonic Studio Piteå, Glasgow, Scotland, pp. 9–16.

Berndt, A. & Hähnel, T. (2010), Modelling Musical Dynamics, *in* 'Audio Mostly 2010: 5th Conf. on Interaction with Sound—Sound and Design', Interactive Institute/Sonic Studio Piteå, ACM, Piteå, Sweden, pp. 134–141.

Bernhard, C. (1667/1999), Von der Singekunst oder -manier, *in* J. Müller-Blattau, ed., 'Die Kompositionslehre Heinrich Schützens in der Fassung seines Schülers Christoph Bernhard', 3rd edn, Bärenreiter. original publication 1667.

Bresin, R. (2001), Articulation Rules for Automatic Music Performance, *in* R. Dannenberg, ed., 'Proc. of the Int. Computer Music Conf. (ICMC)', International Computer Music Association, La Habana, Cuba, pp. 294–297.

Clarke, E. F. (1999), Rhythm and Timing in Music, *in* D. Deutsch, ed., 'The Psychology of Music', 2nd edn, Academic Press, Elsevier, San Diego, CA, USA, chapter 13, pp. 473–500.

Dannenberg, R. B. (2006), The Interpretation of MIDI Velocity, *in* 'Proc. of the Int. Computer Music Conf. (ICMC)', International Computer Music Association, Tulane University, New Orleans, USA, pp. 193–196.

Dannenberg, R. B., Pellerin, H. & Derenyi, I. (1998), A Study of Trumpet Envelopes, *in* 'Proc. of the Int. Computer Music Conf. (ICMC)', International Computer Music Association, San Francisco, USA, pp. 57–61.

de Poli, G. (2004), 'Methodologies for Expressiveness Modelling of and for Music Performance', *Journal of New Music Research* **33**(3), 189–202.

Dixon, S. (2000), Extraction of Musical Performance Parameters from Audio Data, *in* 'Proc. IEEE Pacific-Rim Conf. on Multimedia', IEEE Circuits and Systems Society, IEEE Signal Processing Society, and The Signal & Multimedia Processing Lab, Sydney, Australia, pp. 42–45.

Dixon, S. (2006), Onset Detection Revisited, *in* 'Proc. of the 9th Conf. on Digital Audio Effects (DAFx'06)', CIRMMT, Schulich School of Music/McGill University, Montreal, Canada, pp. 133–137.

Friberg, A. (1995), 'Matching the rule parameters of PHRASE ARCH to performances of "Träumerei": a preliminary study', *Quarterly Progress and Status Report* **36**(2–3), 63–70.

Friberg, A., Bresin, R. & Sundberg, J. (2006), 'Overview of the KTH rule system for musical performance', *Advances in Cognitive Psychology, Special Issue on Music Performance* **2**(2-3), 145–161.

Friberg, A. & Sundberg, J. (1999), 'Does Music Performance Allude to Locomotion? A Model of Final Ritardandi Derived from Measurements of Stopping Runners', *The Journal of the Acoustical Society of America* **105**(3), 1469–1484.

Fyk, J. (1995), *Melodic Intonation, Psychoacoustics, and the Violin*, Organon, Zielona Góra, Poland.

Gabrielsson, A. (1985), 'Interplay Between Analysis and Synthesis in Studies of Music Performance and Music Experience', *Music Perception* **3**(1), 59–86.

Gabrielsson, A., Bengtsson, I. & Gabrielsson, B. (1983), 'Performance of musical rhythm in 3/4 and 6/8 meter', *Scandinavian Journal of Psychology* **24**(1), 193–213.

Gatty, R. (1912), 'Tempo Rubato', *The Musical Times* **53**(829), 160–162.

Goebl, W. (2001), 'Melody lead in piano performance: Expressive device or artifact?', *Journal of the Acoustical Society of America* **110**(1), 563–572.

Goebl, W. (2011), Die ungleichzeitige Gleichzeitigkeit des Spiels: Tempo rubato in Magaloff's Chopin und andere Asynchronizitäten, *in* H. von Loesch & S. Weinzierl, eds, 'Gemessene Interpretation: Computergestützte Aufführungsanalyse im Kreuzverhör der Disziplinen', TU Berlin, Schott Music, Mainz, Germany, chapter 10, pp. 145–156.

Hall, C. V. & O'Donnell, J. T. (2009), Using Regular Expressions to Express Bowing Patterns for String Players, *in* G. Scavone, V. Verfaille & A. da Silva, eds, 'Proc. of the Int. Computer Music Conf. (ICMC)', International Computer Music Association, Schulich School of Music/McGill University, Montreal, Canada, pp. 37–40.

Hefling, S. E. (1993), *Rhythmic Alteration in Seventeenth- and Eighteenth-Century Music. Notes Inégales and Overdotting*, Schirmer Books, New York, NY.

Hähnel, T. (2013), *Baroque performance—a research study on characteristic parameters of 18th Century music*, Vol. 2 of *Studies in Cognitive Musicology*, Electronic Publishing Osnabrück, Osnabrück, Germany.

Hähnel, T. & Berndt, A. (2010), Expressive Articulation for Synthetic Music Performances, *in* 'Proc. of New Interfaces for Musical Expression (NIME) 2010', University of Technology Sydney, Sydney, Australia, pp. 277–282.

Honing, H. (2003), 'The Final Retard: On Music, Motion, and Kinematic Models', *Computer Music Journal* **27**(3), 66–72.

Hudson, R. (1994), *Stolen Time, The History of Tempo Rubato*, Oxford University Press.

Jerkert, J. (2003), Measurements and models of musical articulation, Master's thesis, KTH Royal Institute of Technology, Stockholm, Sweden.

Juslin, P. N. (2009), Emotion in music performance, *in* S. Hallam, I. Cross & M. Thaut, eds, 'The Oxford Handbook of Music Psychology', Oxford University Press, Oxford, chapter 35, pp. 377–389.

Juslin, P. N., Friberg, A. & Bresin, R. (2002), 'Toward a computational model of expression in music performance: the GERM model', *Musicae Scientiea* **5**(1), 63–122.

Madison, G. (2000), On the nature of variability in isochronous serial interval production, *in* P. Desain & L. Windsor, eds, 'Rhythm Perception and Production', Studies on New Music Research, Swets & Zeitlinger, Lisse, The Netherlands, pp. 95–113.

Maempel, H.-J. (2011), Musikaufnahmen als Datenquelle der Interpretationsanalyse, *in* H. von Loesch & S. Weinzierl, eds, 'Gemessene Interpretation: Computergestützte Aufführungsanalyse im Kreuzverhör der Disziplinen', Schott, Mainz, Germany, chapter 11, pp. 157–171.

Maestre, E. & Gómez, E. (2005), Automatic Characterization of Dynamics and Articulation of Expressive Monophonic Recordings, *in* 'Proc. of the 118th Audio Engineering Society Convention', Audio Engineering Society (AES), Barcelona, Spain.

Parncutt, R. (2003), Accents and expression in piano performance, *in* K. W. Niemöller, ed., 'Perspektiven und Methoden einer Systematischen Musikwissenschaft', Peter Lang, Frankfurt/Main, Germany, pp. 163–185. Festschrift Fricke.

Quantz, J. J. (1752), *Versuch einer Anweisung, die Flöte traversière zu spielen*, Bärenreiter. Reprint (1997), H. Augsbach.

Ramirez, R., Hazan, A. & Maestre, E. (2005), Intra-Note Features Prediction Model for Jazz Saxophone Performance, *in* 'Proc. of the Int. Computer Music Conf. (ICMC)', International Computer Music Association, Universitat Pompeu Fabra, Barcelona, Spain.

Rasch, R. A. (1979), 'Synchronisation in Performed Ensemble Music', *Acustica* **43**, 121–131.

Repp, B. H. (1992), 'Diversity and Commonality in Music Performance: An Analysis of Timing Microstructure in Schumann's "Träumerei"', *Journal of the Acoustical Society of America* **92**(5), 2546–2568.

Riemann, H. (1884), *Musikalische Dynamik und Agogik: Lehrbuch der musikalischen Phrasirung auf Grund einer Revision der Lehre von der musikalischen Metrik und Rhythmik*, D. Rahter, Hamburg, Germany.

Shaffer, H. (1981), 'Performances of Chopin, Bach and Bartok: Studies in Motor Programming', *Cognitive Psychology* **13**, 326–376.

Sundberg, J. & Verrillo, V. (1980), 'On the Anatomy of the Retard: A Study of Timing in Music', *The Journal of the Acoustical Society of America* **68**(3), 772–779.

Todd, N. P. M. (1995), 'The Kinematics of Musical Expression', *The Journal of the Acoustical Society of America* **97**(3), 1940–1949.

Vienna Symphonic Library GmbH (2015), 'Vienna Symphonic Library', https://vsl.co.at/de [last visited: May 2015]. Sample library of orchestral instruments.

Yamada, M. (1998), Temporal fluctuation in musical performances: Fluctuations caused by the limitation of performers' controllability and by artistic expression, *in* S. W. Yi, ed., 'Proc. of the 5th Int. Conf. on Music Perception and Cognition', Western Music Research Institute, Seoul National University, Seoul, South Korea, pp. 353–358.

Axel Berndt, Tilo Hähnel Chapter 5

# Studying Music Performance and Perception via Interaction

**Abstract** Musicians achieve expression in their performance to a large part by using holistic concepts. Likewise, many aspects of expression are perceived unconsciously by listeners. For performance research and the development of models for synthetic music performance the challenge lies in uncovering the underlying principles of a widely undiscovered interplay between several parameters like timing, dynamics, and articulation. Inégalité is a typical example for this. Simply put, the impression of inégalité in musical pulse refers to an unequal playing of notes of equal value. This involves the full range of performance aspects and complex interdependencies between them. Novel interactive techniques for performance synthesis open up new possibilities to study these performance aspects and interdependencies more effectively. We demonstrate this by a study that addresses inégalité, in which experts and non-experts interactively adjusted the performance of a short musical phrase. The results give insight into the relationships of different performance parameters and they give rise to discussing the role of expertise and skill. With this chapter, we exemplify and hope to inspire music-related research methods that are driven by new interactive music techniques.

## 5.1 Introduction

Conveying the impression of liveliness in a synthetic music performance requires a vital work with performance features, such as timing, dynamics, and articulation. Techniques for the synthesis of expressive music performances have been developed for several decades now and they had a first peak in the 1980s when Todd (1985) presented his "Model of Expressive Timing in Tonal Music". Computer-based expressive performance techniques are based on machine learning techniques (Widmer, Flossmann & Grachten 2009), mathematical models (Todd 1985, 1989, Mazzola, Göller & Müller 2002), and rule systems (Friberg, Bresin & Sundberg 2006). An introduction and overview of the subject is given by Widmer & Goebl (2004) and also Hähnel (2013) and Berndt (2011*b*). One aim of performance research in this context is the search for appropriate models and parameterizations to describe performance features, detect typicalities in human performances, and be able to synthesize human-like performances. This may then lead to better tools for computer-based music production.

However, the parameter space that is spanned by musical performance features is high-dimensional. An analysis by measuring human recordings (Gabrielsson 1999) is usually confronted with an ambiguous interplay of several layers of features of which a single one is hard to isolate. Instead, listener studies can be performed in the following way. Based on deliberately produced musical material, listeners judge performances and, thus, provide clues for the underlying research question (Gabrielsson 1985). But even this approach is limited, since human musicians intuitively perform many features, over which they have only limited control. It is extremely hard, if not impossible, for most musicians to consciously form, e.g. a linear and an exponential ritardando. With synthesized musical material it is much easier to vary such parameters with finest nuances, as fine as the research question and stimulus design for a study demands. The number of stimuli and the length of such a study are, however, limited for practical reasons.

At this point interactive music techniques come into play. Participants can interactively explore the parameter space and adjust certain performance features according to a given task. In contrast to a mere listening study the participants are now actively involved. They decide about the necessity and degree of settings and their gradual refinement. Thereby, a much wider parameter space can be covered. In the study described below we could effectively cover a three-dimensional parameter space, 21 grades per parameter, in sum 9,261 different stimuli. This exemplary study addresses a performance phenomenon called "Inégalité".

The succeeding section provides an introduction to this phenomenon and related research. The technical background and methodology are described in Section 5.4. Interdependencies between different parameters are uncovered in Section 5.5. It turned out that the ability of identifying the performance parameters is an important aspect and has an effect on the responses. Section 5.6 includes a discussion of the results, e.g. the correlation of different parameters and the effects of expertise. This chapter compiles the results of an interdisciplinary project which involves computer science and musicology, previously presented by Hähnel & Berndt (2011*a*,*b*).

## 5.2 Inégalité and Performance Research

The note inégale—or, generally speaking, the unequal playing of notes, which is also connected to the phenomenon of overdotting—is an object of investigation for musicians, music historians, ethnomusicologists, musicologists with empirical interest and computer scientists. Following paragraphs include a brief description of notes inégales as a central element of micro timing phenomena from different perspectives: performance practice and empirical musicology. The various approaches with which notes inégales were studied led to a broad knowledge base, which provides the foundation for the hypotheses formatted afterwards.

### 5.2.1 Historically Informed Performance

In the middle of the 20th century, an increasing number of musicians interested in "early music" rediscovered the historical and geographical differences in performance practises of European art music and formed the Historically Informed Performance (HIP) movement (Butt 2002). The focus on performance aspects is related to a more general turn towards performance, which became increasingly notable in the middle of the 20th century and which can be linked to the concept of "performativity", which the linguist John L. Austin (1962) introduced.

The increasing interest in performance took also place in other arts, like performance art, happenings or action paintings, where the process of the creation gets more important than the outcome. And they were highly influential on a number of research fields. Therefore, Hinrichsen (2011) detected a "performative turn" in musicology, too.

Today, the HIP movement has a history of its own. Changes of performance aesthetics and interpretations of early music are valuable sources for research in the history of music performances, as well as in music psychology and sociology. Among the most regarded sources of German performance practice of the 18th century were the treatises of Leopold Mozart, Johann Joachim Quantz, and Carl

Philipp Emanuel Bach. They also prescribe micro timing deviations to stress the beats in a measure, particularly when it comes to French music, from where the term inégalité was borrowed.

> "Ich muß hierbey eine nothwendige Anmerkung machen, welche die Zeit, wie lange jede Note gehalten werden muß, betrifft. [...] Die Hauptnoten müssen allezeit [...] mehr erhoben werden als die durchgehenden. Dieser Regel zu Folge müssen die geschwindesten Noten, in einem jeden Stücke von mäßigem Tempo, oder auch im Adagio, ungeachtet sie dem Gesichte nach einerley Geltung haben, dennoch ein wenig ungleich gespielet werden: so daß man die anschlagenden Noten einer jeden Figur, nämlich die erste, dritte, fünfte und siebente, etwas länger anhält, und achte: doch muss dieses Anhalten nicht soviel ausmachen, als wenn Puncte dabey stünden."[1]
>
> Here I must make a necessary observation concerning the length of time each note must be held. [...] [T]he principal notes always must be emphasized more than the passing. In consequence of this rule, the quickest notes in every piece of *moderate tempo*, or even in the *Adagio*, though they seem to have the same value, namely the first, third, fifth, and seventh, are held slightly longer than the passing [...], although this lengthening must not be as much as if the notes were dotted.[2]

Notes inégales, in the strict historical sense, are an emphasis of metrical accents, which are, in most cases, the beats. Short notes that fall on the beat are protracted, whereas notes between the beats start later and are therefore contracted to the same amount. Since both are coupled with each other, the protractions and contractions compensate each other.

### 5.2.2 Analysing Music as Performed

About the same time, when musicians started investigating historical differences in performance practice and showed an increased interest in micro timing phenomena, ethnomusicologists discovered the potential of micro timing, too. However, their approaches were more related to the relatively new field

[1] Quantz (1752), page 105.
[2] Quantz (2001), page 123.

of computer science. In 1967, Bengtsson (1970) proposed that computers allow for the analysis of music as it is performed, providing the possibility of directly obtaining digital performance data. The advent of computers opened up new possibilities for music research, particularly with an ethnological perspective. Rhythmical proportions as they are notated can be seen as rhythm classes rather than precise temporal information.

From their observations, Bengtson and his colleagues derived the concept of "systematic deviations", which describes the deviation of measured time proportions from rhythm classes. These deviations depend on musical structure, tradition, and individuality. The focus on rhythm made clear that micro timing, which refers to systematic deviations below the measure-level, is a key to understand performance traditions and musical dialects.

The majority of performance analyses following Bengtson's approach concentrated on timing. Gabrielsson (1999) found various degrees of differences between notes of equal value among Swedish folk songs and the Viennese Waltz. Similar phenomena were discovered in more remote cultures, as Gerischer (2003) demonstrated, or in diverse Western music styles, as analyzed by Langner (2002). Though these micro deviations were already known, the novelty was that, due to technological developments, these deviations can be observed scientifically in larger amounts and finer detail.

However, reducing notes inégales to a question of onset timing alone would be wrong, although onset timing seems to be the most important aspect. By altering the playing technique, like the bowing on string instruments, onset times are affected as well as loudness, timbre, tone duration, and many other parameters. While playing notes inégales, these parameters cannot be decoupled from each other. From a musician's point of view this might even be unnecessary. However, gaining insight into the complex interplay of the different parameters and human perception requires an in-depth analysis.

Fabian & Schubert (2008) made a first step in this direction. They investigated interdependencies between different timing features on the perception of note ratios in dotted notes. Similar to notes inégales, overdotted notes that fall on the beat are prolonged. Under certain circumstances, such as in French Overtures, they can be played like double-dotted notes. The similarity of the so-called overdotting and inégalité is described in detail by Hefling (1993). The approach of Fabian & Schubert (2008) was new, since most micro timing analyses concentrated only on the onset times of tones.

Fabian & Schubert (2008) particularly analyzed how tone onset time, tone duration, and mean tempo affect the perception of "dottedness" in Variation No. 7 of Bach's "Goldberg Variations". One study included a listening test in which the participants were presented synthetic performances of dotted notes. The stimuli varied in a combination of onset timing, tempo, and tone duration. The time ratio of the three tones (dotted note, following short note and normal eighth note) was either like a dotted $(0.75 : 0.25 : 0.5)$ or double-dotted $(0.875 : 0.125 : 0.5)$ note, the tempo was slow or fast, and the tone duration was threefold: overall legato, first-note staccato, or third-note staccato. Although each of the three independent factors had only two levels, onset timing and tone duration had a great influence on the perception of "dottedness". The most striking result was that the faster the tempo and the shorter the tone duration, the more dotted the rhythm appeared to the listeners. These results can be transferred to notes inégales, since both are strongly related (Hefling 1993)

Nevertheless, there are still some problems. Firstly, the three factors onset timing, tone duration and mean tempo are all temporal factors. Referring to original sources, like Quantz's (1752) treatise on flute playing, inégalité (as well as overdotting) always includes aspects of loudness and articulation. Secondly, tempo largely affects the main character of a piece of music and also affects the perception of meter. An allegro is likely to be perceived as alla breve, which means that the half notes are perceived as beats. On the contrary, the pulse in an Adagio can refer to eighth notes. All these changes are categorical and it is hard to imagine that the same composition does not change its character of expression when played in a very different tempo. Since overdotting and notes inégales depend on the character of the composition, tempo is highly influential a priori. Any study design that ignores this relationship by comparing different tempi as if they would not involve anything but a tempo change, are problematic. A tempo change touches a different topic and should be left constant to ensure proper experimental conditions. Finally, discretizing the independent parameters to three steps seems to be a good choice. This offers several combinatorial possibilities. However, a finer discretization of at least ten steps per parameter affords a preciser outcome.

The exemplary study that is described in this chapter takes account of the historical view and investigates inégalité as a phenomenon, of which onset timing, tone duration, and loudness are three dimensions of its entirety. The main questions are: Are onset timing, tone duration and loudness means to affect the perception of inégalité in eighth notes? Are they interdependent? Does expertise influence the perception of and preference for the degree of inégalité?

## 5.3 Hypotheses

From the foregoing considerations we assume that in notes inégales, onset timing, loudness, and tone duration are used to emphasize a tone. If each of the parameters has an effect on the perceived degree of inégalité, this effect should be increased when all parameters are used simultaneously. To avoid an overemphasis, the intense use of one parameter should imply a rather moderate use of the others. These considerations led to the following hypotheses.

1. When controlled separately, the parameters of loudness, timing, and duration are used to a larger extent than in combination.
2. Assuming an interdependency between and somehow interchangeability of the parameters, there should be a negative correlation between all parameters when used in combination.
3. The results are more distinct, if not only significant for participants who are experts. Experts should also be more correct in identifying a parameter by listening.

Following Gabrielsson (1985) a further question was whether specialized performers or listeners prefer a different degree of inégalité than non-specialists.

There are two contradictory hypotheses regarding expertise. Experts may prefer a higher degree of inégalité, because they are used to it, as Gabrielsson (1985) showed for inequality of beat length in the Viennese Waltz. On the other hand, it is also possible that non-experts intuitively prefer a degree of inégalité of a similar intensity, because the macro timing is not affected and the inequality of eighths notes is used in a wide range of styles, right up to Jazz music's swinging eighth notes. As a consequence of these contradictory hypotheses, the investigation of expertise is rather exploratory than hypothesis-driven.

## 5.4 Methodology

The analysis-by-synthesis approach that this study is based on reaches back to Metfessel (1926) and Seashore (1932). It was detailed by Bengtsson & Gabrielsson (1977). Various stimuli are presented to listeners, who were then asked to judge them. These stimuli comprized synthetic performances that differed in the characteristic of some particular performance parameters. For the present study this approach has been modified for the following reason. The total amount of stimuli depends largely on the number of grades a parameter is subdivided into. A combination of three parameters of 21 grades each, as in this study, results in $21^3 = 9,261$ stimuli, which are practically impossible to be all presented to the listeners. The problem was to provide all stimuli but at the same time reduce them to a minimum. This was solved by letting the participants manipulate these three parameters independently and interactively until they approved the parameter combination they preferred. The whole procedure, the participants and the technical setup are described in the following sections.

### 5.4.1 Participants

In order to analyze the expertise of the participants, diverse skills were captured in more detail. It was important to test musicians with advanced skills and knowledge about the Baroque performance of notes inégales. Hence, the test included musicologists, musicians, music teachers, and professional musicians specialized in Historically Informed Performance.

The participants were 36 western socialized adults (21 female, 15 male). To ascertain their expertise they were asked for how many years they were playing an instrument, whether they had a degree in music, musicology, music education, or similar subjects, how much they liked classical and Baroque music, and whether they were working as professional musicians. The answers were used in the later analysis to test which expertise influenced particular results most.

10 participants were professional musicians, 16 had a degree in music, 20 played an instrument for more than 10 years, 14 of which for more than 20 years. 25 stated to like classical music or Baroque music in particular. 22 were acquainted with the term Historically Informed Performance.

### 5.4.2 Stimulus Design

The stimulus comprised the first four bars of a Polonoise composed by Georg Philipp Telemann, shown in figure 5.1. Two tests were carried out, first a *separate parameter test* and then a *combined parameter test*. In the first test the participants were asked to modify the performance of the eighth notes of the stimulus, which was presented in a playback loop. Either timing (esp. rubato), dynamics (esp. metrical accentuation), or articulation (focussing on tone duration changes) were modified (refer to section 5.4.3 in this book for further details of the parameters and their implementation), i.e., only one parameter was set modifiable at

**Figure 5.1:** The first four bars of the Polonoise taken from the overture in d-major "La Galliarde" TWV 55:D13 for strings & b.c., composed by Georg Philipp Telemann. This was used as the stimulus, performed in a playback loop.

once. With the Arrow-Up key the eighth notes on the beat (□ in figure 5.1) were emphasized. A decrease of this emphasis or even an emphasis of the eighths between the beats (△ in figure 5.1) was set by pressing the Arrow-Down key. If the limit of the parameter spectrum was reached, a beep sound signalled that no further modification was possible in this direction.

The first test included two tasks: first, the participants were asked to identify the means, by which they emphasized the notes, i.e., to identify the parameter they manipulate. Then they had to tune the relation of the eighths as they supposed to sound best and confirm their configuration with the Enter key. The participants were not influenced by a visual feedback indicating the parameter value. They only saw the score including the squares and triangles as shown in figure 5.1 and, therefore, depended completely on the auditory feedback.

In the second test the same stimulus was presented to the participants who now had the task to tune all three parameters independently. All parameters were set by an array of the six control-keys above the arrow keys on standard computer keyboards. These were labelled with up and down arrows in red, black and blue. In this test the participants were handed an instruction referring to the parameters and the keys as shown in figure 5.2.

### 5.4.3 Technical Setup

Offering control over particular performance parameters raises a nontrivial modeling problem. No performance feature can be regarded as isolated. For instance, the loudness of each tone in a performance does not result from only one

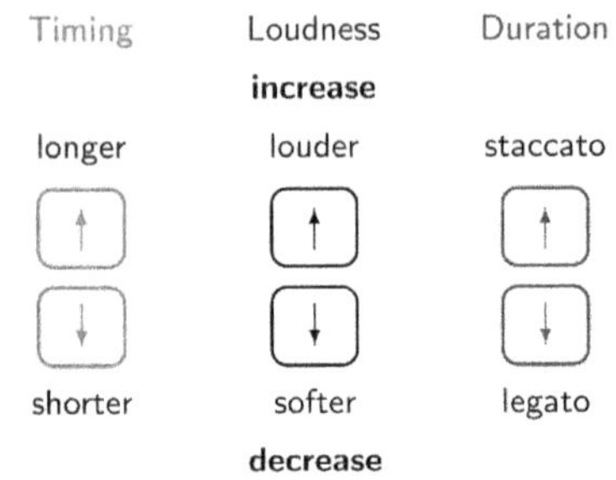


**Figure 5.2:** Instructions for the modification of non-beat eighth notes.

aspect of dynamics but from a complex interplay of several of them. If an interaction intends to affect only one feature, say articulation, we nonetheless need to know about the whole interplay and the contribution of the particular feature. Formally, expressive performance can be regarded as a series of transformations that is applied to a musical composition. We distinguish the three categories timing, dynamics, and articulation. Here, we introduce them only very briefly, for a comprehensive description please refer to chapter 4 in this book.

**Timing** maps symbolic time (score timing) onto physical time (usually in milliseconds). It comprizes several layers of timing features, i.e. tempo (macro timing), rubato (self-compensating micro deviations), asynchrony (between parts in a polyphonic setting), and random imprecision (Berndt & Hähnel 2009, Berndt 2011*a*).

**Dynamics** sets the loudness of each musical event. We distinguish macro dynamics (the basic loudness function of the musical piece) and two micro layers that introduce fine deviations to the basic loudness, metrical accentuations and articulations (only the loudness aspect of the latter) (Berndt & Hähnel 2010).

**Articulation** shapes each individual musical event (note) according to its loudness, duration, envelope, and timbre (Hähnel & Berndt 2010, Hähnel 2010).

Based on theory, analyses of human performances and studies with expert musicians, we developed mathematical models for a huge corpus of performance features including all the above mentioned. The flexible parameterization of the feature models allows for a huge bandwidth of characteristics, including those that could be observed in performances by human musicians, and even atypical ones that are more of theoretical interest. Most models even allow the definition of new instances, e.g. new articulations, time signature-based accentuation schemes, and rubato patterns.

We have designed an XML-based high-level description language and implemented the models in a performance rendering engine. Different performances can be described and are stored as performance styles. Together with a "raw" MIDI file (MIDI Manufacturers Association 1996) these performance styles are rendered into expressive MIDI sequences.

The rendering process is fast enough to allow the re-rendering of a musical piece even during its playback. This fulfills the requirement of responsiveness to introduce interactivity, i.e., to change over to other performance styles and, thereby create style combinations. The performance engine then automatically creates musically plausible, seamless transitions by simulating the reactions of musicians with an agent-based approach (Berndt 2010). This concept is based on the assumption that musicians aggregate note sequences to figures and phrases rather than playing each note separately. This is underpinned by the fact that a central aim of expressive performance is to reflect compositional structure. The same accounts for orchestration which deals with performance aspects, too (Sevsay 2005). Based on this, we implemented interactive virtual musicians, each representing a MIDI channel and able to change certain performance features. These interaction-driven changes are aligned with structural features like sections, phrases, figures/motifs, and measures to create musically more plausible performances than simple hard switches would do and strengthen the musical coherence.

This flexibility and full control over any performance detail, even the most subtle, makes our performance engine a very useful tool especially for musicological and psychological experiments and studies. Its application programming interface (API) provides any application with interactive control over the music performance just like in the case of the study described in this chapter. The participants had to explore a domain of possibilities and find a parameter setting that matches their preferences. The setup is shown in figure 5.3.

### 5.4.4 Feature Manipulation

Our performance synthesis techniques are MIDI-based which comes along with the advantages of the MIDI format, like modularity. We can use it with any

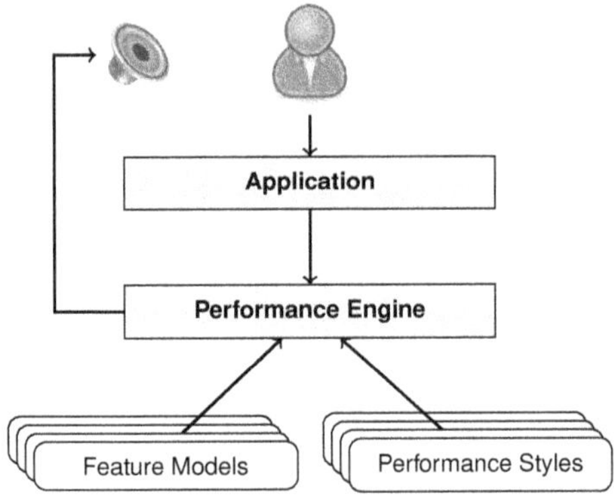


**Figure 5.3:** The setup of the study.

available sound synthesis module that reads MIDI messages. We chose the software sampler *VSampler 3* (Speedsoft 2006) as it runs smoothly even on weak machines and laptops. The quality of the instrumental sounds is reasonable, it is not high-end quality, though. This trade-off made the study mobile and gave us the flexibility to easily approach experts at different locations and from different cities.

The application program gave the participants of the study control over certain parameters of the music performance, comprising timing (esp. rubato), dynamics (esp. metrical accentuation), and articulation (focussing on tone duration changes). The interface is shown in Figure 5.2. The parameter space for the performance maps to the controller states. It was discretized into 21 steps for each controller ranging from -10 (minimal setting) to 10 (maximal setting). It was important for the study to cover not just plausible settings, i.e., settings that create typical performances of the used musical material as known from most CD productions and from literature on Historically Informed Performance, but also include the border regions and implausible settings. This is a unique feature of the present study as the vast majority of traditional studies of this kind are limited to static (non-interactive) auditory stimuli, all of which have to be presented to the listener.

**Rubato** is a timing distortion that is self-compensating within a certain timeframe (Goebl 2011, Hudson 2004). According to this definition the average tempo over that timeframe remains unchanged regardless of the intensity

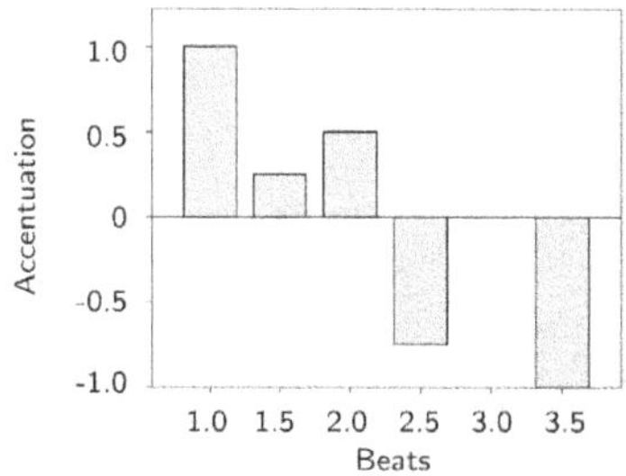


**Figure 5.4:** The accentuation scheme was scaled interactively.

of the rubato distortion. The basic tempo of the music in the study was 120 bpm. The rubato frame was of quarter note length and it was repeatedly applied to the whole music. The distortion was modelled by a power function in the unity square. The timing relation between the first and the second eighth can be described as follows.

$$\left((0.5^i)\,0.98 : (1-0.5^i)\,0.98\right) \quad | \quad i \in [0.4, 1.6]$$

Via the respective controller the participants were setting the value of i which was linearly interpolated from $-10 \rightarrow (i = 1.6)$ to $10 \rightarrow (i = 0.4)$. The most positive controller values created a swing-like timing. Negative values inverted this characteristic.

**Metrical accentuation** is a micro dynamics feature. It defines an accentuation scheme, i.e., a loudness contour as shown in Figure 5.4 that is applied to each measure. The participants were able to scale this scheme from -60 to 60 MIDI velocity units. Positive values created most plausible accentuations though an extreme positive setting covered a range of 107 MIDI velocity units causing a pianissimo for the softest and a fortissimo for the strongest accentuations. This was, of course, over-accentuation. Negative controller values inverted the scheme.

**Articulation** is a complex phenomenon that affects all parameters of a tone, like duration, loudness, envelope, and timbre. In this study the articulation controller was steering only the duration allowing tight legati up to very short staccati. This creates either a cantabile or a rhythmically pronounced performance. However, the behavior of articulation settings was even more complex. The duration of each second eighth note under a quarter beat decreased faster than the first so that the emphatic relation between both shifts accordingly. Three sample points were defined (see table 5.1) and linearly interpolated.

| controller state | Duration of 1st eighth | 2nd eighth |
|---|---|---|
| 10 | 0.35 | 0.2 |
| 0 | 0.7 | 0.4 |
| -10 | 1.0 | 1.0 |

**Table 5.1:** The key data of the articulation settings.

The positive controller settings for rubato and metrical accentuation cover the scope that could be observed within human performances. Negative settings create inverse characteristics. This does not apply to articulation, of course, since negative durations are practically impossible.

In the separate parameter test (first test) the controllers were randomly initialized at the extremes, i.e. -10 or 10. In the combined parameter test (second test) the initialization was also random but over the full parameter ranges. All manipulations could be done directly while the music was playing. The performance engine updated the performance within a latency frame of 500 milliseconds after interaction. This inertia allowed the engine to collect multiple inputs and align the changes with the next beat or barline to produce a more homogeneous musical output.

Furthermore, the system tracked all interactions. The protocol recorded the time of interaction and the controller settings. At the end of the test the users had to approve the settings. The complete test duration was protocolled as well. This allows insights into how the users explored the search space and how long they listened to certain settings until they made a decision and interaction.

## 5.5 Results

The study turned out to be more difficult for the subjects than expected. Therefor, 11 participants had to be excluded from the second task. The remaining 25 participants included 19, who had been playing an instrument for more than 10 years, 15 with a degree in a music related subject and 10 professional musicians.

| | | all | instr. | | degr. | | music. | |
|---|---|---|---|---|---|---|---|---|
| | | | yes | no | yes | no | yes | no |
| | $\Sigma$ | 36 | 20 | 16 | 16 | 20 | 10 | 26 |
| **Timing** | correct | 21 | 12 | 9 | 8 | 13 | 6 | 15 |
| | ambivalent | 7 | 5 | 2 | 5 | 2 | 4 | 3 |
| | incorrect | 8 | 3 | 5 | 3 | 5 | 0 | 8 |
| | $\chi^2$ | — | 1.792 | | 2.563 | | 6.092 | |
| | $p$ | — | 0.383 | | 0.336 | | 0.053 | |
| **Loudness** | correct | 15 | 11 | 4 | 8 | 7 | 7 | 8 |
| | ambivalent | 2 | 1 | 1 | 1 | 1 | 1 | 1 |
| | incorrect | 19 | 8 | 11 | 7 | 12 | 2 | 17 |
| | $\chi^2$ | — | 3.337 | | 0.950 | | 5.979 | |
| | $p$ | — | 0.193 | | 0.740 | | 0.051 | |
| **Duration** | correct | 17 | 12 | 5 | 9 | 8 | 7 | 10 |
| | ambivalent | 7 | 5 | 2 | 5 | 2 | 3 | 4 |
| | incorrect | 12 | 3 | 9 | 2 | 10 | 0 | 12 |
| | $\chi^2$ | — | 6.808 | | 6.311 | | 6.930 | |
| | $p$ | — | 0.032 | | 0.049 | | 0.030 | |

**Table 5.2:** Parameter identification: Different kinds of experts are compared to non-experts with a $\chi^2$ test; instr.: participants playing an instrument for $> 10$ years; degr.: participants with a degree in a music-related subject; music.: professional musicians.

### 5.5.1 Separate Parameter Test

The answers given in the first task were collected and classified manually. Possible answers could be correct, ambivalent, or incorrect. A correct answer had to be unambiguous. In some cases this was difficult because the term "length" is ambivalent—it might refer to the length of the inter-onset interval (timing) or the tone duration. "Length" was classified as correct for articulation only if the timing parameter was undoubtedly distinguished and vice versa, e.g., in the combination of "length" and "articulation" or "tempo" and "length". It was otherwise classified as ambivalent. When a participant gave the answer "length" in at least two cases, he or she was asked if there was a difference between the two kinds of lengths. If no difference could be made, both answers were classified as ambivalent. Table 5.2 gives the results of the answers given in the first task.

In the separate parameter test, controller values, which the participants tuned in for each of the three parameters, did not show a normal distribution, as the results of a Kolmogorov-Smirnov test and Shapiro-Wilk test showed. The deviation from a normal distribution was particularly problematic for timing. To find the reason for this deviation, an investigation of the tuning process showed that some participants barely used the arrow-keys before confirming their decision. Thus, the question was raised whether the participants did explore the parameter spectrum sufficiently enough to get a notion of the possibilities they had—it was also hardly possible to identify the parameter correctly if the participants had not modified it to a certain degree. Therefore, we excluded data when the modification range during the test was below seven, regardless of the value finally approved. Under this condition four timing samples and two duration samples were excluded. The remaining samples showed a normal distribution and could be used for statistical analyses described in the following.

### 5.5.2 Combined Parameter Test

In the second test, timing was the parameter the participants modified most. Figure 5.5(c) shows the distribution of the number of controller events recorded before the approval for each of the parameters separately. Since the data were, again, not normally distributed, differences were tested with the Friedman test. It showed that the differences between the three groups were significant at the $\alpha = 0.001$ level. Thus, there was a significant difference of the number of controller events made before the approval between the three parameters.

### 5.5.3 Hypothesis 1: Differences

The sample pairs of the controller values taken from the separate and combined parameter test were tested for timing, loudness, and duration. A t-test and a Levine-test could not reveal a significant difference between the parameter tunings in the two tests, in which the parameters were tuned separately and in combination. Figures 5.5(a) and 5.5(b) show the results of the controller values for both tests.

### 5.5.4 Hypothesis 2: Correlations

Timing and loudness were negatively correlated. The Pearson correlation coefficient of $r = -0.653$ was significant at the $\alpha = 0.001$ level. The plot in figure 5.5(d) shows every sample pair of timing and loudness values, and a regression line to illustrate the correlation. No correlation was found between duration and any of the two remaining parameters.

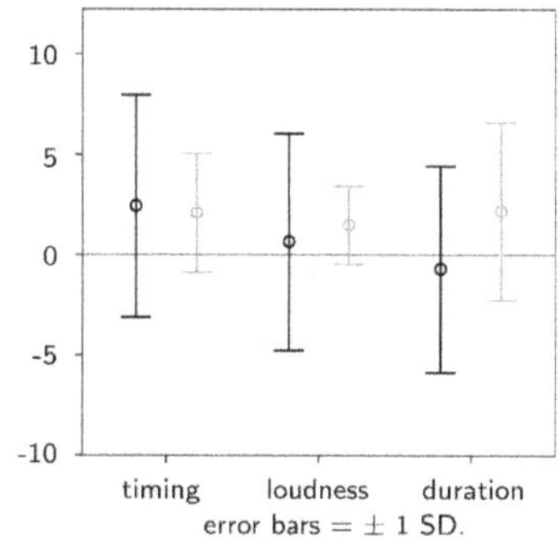


(a) Tunings in the separate parameter test. Values tuned by participants identifying parameters correctly (gray bars) compared to others (black bars).

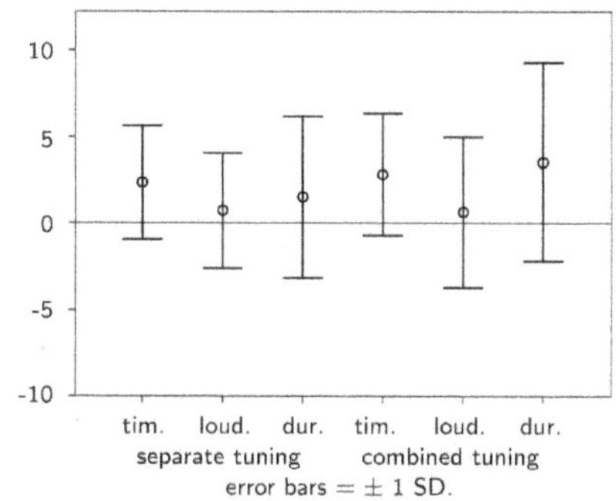


(b) No significant differences between parameters tuned separately or in combination.

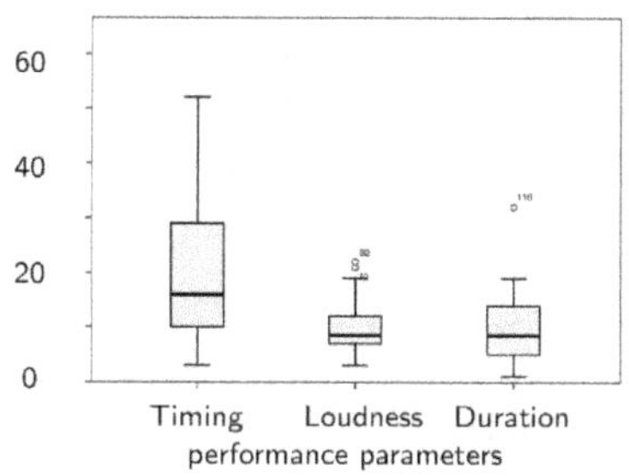


(c) Amount of modulations for each of the three parameters during the combined parameter test.

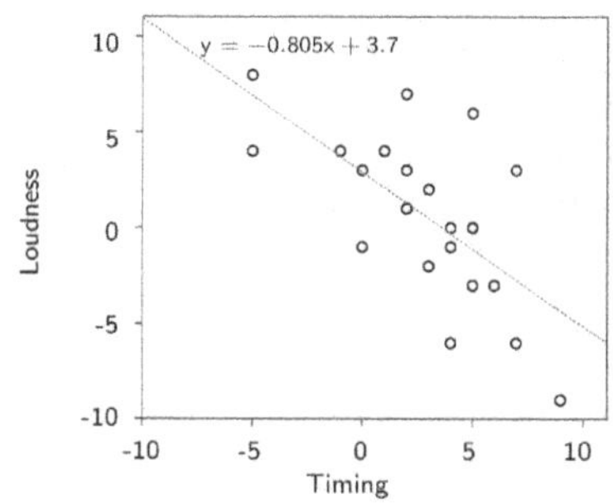


(d) The regression line indicates the negative correlation between timing and loudness tunings.

**Figure 5.5:** Results of the study.

### 5.5.5 Hypothesis 3: Expertise

The influence of expertise on the parameter identification was analyzed with a $\chi^2$ test. The results are listed in table 5.2. Expertise had only an influence on the identification of duration. However, there are at least two considerations to be made. First, participants with a degree in a music-related subject are to the better half represented in the group of participants playing an instrument for

| | Gender | N | Mean | SD | ANOVA F | p |
|---|---|---|---|---|---|---|
| loudness | women | 20 | **3.00** | 4.801 | 7.777 | 0.009 |
| | men | 13 | **-1.31** | 3.473 | | |
| timing | women | 15 | **1.74** | 3.679 | 4.526 | 0.042 |
| | men | 17 | **0.46** | 2.537 | | |

**Table 5.3:** Differences between participants in the separate parameter test.

more than 10 years. And second, professional musicians are both a subgroup of participants playing an instrument for more than 10 years and participants with a degree in music. Only the professional musicians missed the significance for the remaining parameters.

The influence of personal factors (including the expertise factors) on the distribution and mean values of the controller values were analyzed with an ANOVA and a Levine-test. No significant difference of mean values and variances of the controller data was found between experts and non-experts. Curiously, in the separate controller test gender had an effect on duration and timing, which is shown in Table 5.3.

Another group of experts was discovered by a comparison between participants who could identify the parameters and those who could not. Although the mean values did not differ significantly, there was a significant difference in variances of timing and loudness, as shown in table 5.4. These differences are also plotted in figure 5.5(a).

| | Correct | N | Mean | SD | Levine-Test F | p |
|---|---|---|---|---|---|---|
| loudness | no* | 20 | 0.65 | **5.40** | 13.831 | 0.001 |
| | yes | 15 | 1.47 | **1.96** | | |
| timing | no | 7 | 2.43 | **5.53** | 5.478 | 0.026 |
| | yes* | 25 | 2.08 | **2.97** | | |

**Table 5.4:** Levine-test of equal variances. Results of participants correctly identifying the parameter they are tuning show a smaller standard deviation (SD). * include ambivalent answers.

## 5.6 General Discussion

According to the rules of Historically Informed Performance, notes inégales that fall on the beat should be played louder, whereas notes between the beats should be softer, but also later and clearly detached from the following note. Hence, in the present study all parameters for timing, loudness, and duration should be tuned in a positive direction. Indeed, the mean values of all three parameters were positive, as figure 5.5(b) shows. There were no differences of mean values between experts and non-experts. Despite the similarity of mean values, experts showed a much lower variance than non-experts. There are at least two interpretations of these findings. The first explanation is that the large variance that non-experts showed may imply that they do not have a clear idea of shaping a performance. However, the second conclusion implies the equal means. Even when they did not know exactly what they did, the participants were still more likely to choose a parameter setting similar to the experts.

There are three results which might be discussed in more detail. First, timing was the most frequently used performance parameter to gain the impression of inégalité, but the extent of the timing parameter did not differ significantly from loudness and tone duration. This indicates that timing was probably the parameter with which the participants had most difficulties. Until the participants approved their timing adjustment they pressed the arrow-keys about twice as much as they did for loudness and duration. Interestingly, timing was also the parameter most participants identified correctly. This seems to contradict the assumption that the participants had more difficulties with it than with the other parameters. The intense use of the timing adjustments may also result from the fact that timing was the first parameter used in the test. Thus, it is likely that participants used the timing parameter to become acquainted with the task and get a feeling for the available parameter range. It remains unclear whether this playful approach contributed to the correctness of justification or not, but this can be a proper explanation. A separate test of this hypothesis should furnish some interesting aspects of interfaces being as goal-directed as intuitive.

Second, timing and loudness seem to be cumulative, for they were negatively correlated; on the other hand, the extent of performance parameters did not differ between the separate and combined parameter test. These outcomes seem to be contradictory at first glance. However, they are not. While the correlation refers to parameter pairs, the mean values refer to the distribution of all values independently. The negative correlation confirms that participants increasing the timing parameter are quite likely to decrease the loudness parameter. Timing and loudness are therefore like two elements that balance each other out. An equal mean value does not conflict with this explanation. On the contrary, it indicates that both, timing and loudness, are equal means for the degree of inégalité. It only remains unclear whether one of both is dominant. Furthermore, timing and loudness may be interchangeable.

Third, there were no differences between experts and non-experts referring to the statements they made. The variance in the separate controller test, however, differed between those participants who identified the parameter correctly by listening and those participants who failed. Furthermore, the only personal factor with an effect on the results was gender. These results were less expected. Of course, participants who identified parameters by listening correctly clearly showed a smaller variance for timing and loudness.

The ability to identify the parameters correctly turned out being a factor of expertise. Moreover, this ability was the most influencing factor but at the same time it was not linked to any other expertise factor. The results in table 5.2 are non-significant but the effect seems to be big enough to be the basis for further studies, the design of which addresses these questions more directly. No professional musician failed in identifying timing and only two failed in loudness identification. Therefore, the group of professional musicians gained a much higher $\chi^2$ and a much lower $p$ value than the other groups. This may lead to a hypothesis of a twofold expertise: a motor expertise and a knowledge expertise. Participants with a degree in music related subjects, e.g. musicologists, have an expert knowledge in terms of a declarative knowledge but may lack motor skills (simply because of a lack of time to practise etc.). Participants playing an instrument for more than 10 or 20 years clearly have motor skills but may lack certain detailed knowledge about special topics like Historically Informed Performance when they are nonprofessionals. Both groups did not differ from other participants (see table 5.2).

Professional musicians who are specialized in HIP have multiple skills: (i) the ability to internally repeat the motion observed in the stimulus, (ii) detailed declarative knowledge about performance parameters, and (iii) knowledge about where to apply certain characteristics on a particular piece of music regarding information from historical sources. As students of early music orally told, the conscious decomposition of these performance parameters is part of the training at the department of early music of the UdK in Berlin. And experts are also acquainted with these parameters that are important aspects in the whole HIP discourse.

The crucial aspect of motor planning and motor control is known at least since Clynes & Walker (1982) and Shaffer (1981). In their view, a motor program allows storing a single movement which consists of temporal and spatial parameters. Applied on an instrument, these movements cause certain effects on timing, loudness, and articulation. In a similar way these parameters seem to be perceived as a whole rather than as a combination of different parameters. Only the group of professional musicians, which assumedly have internal representations of the movements simulated in the stimuli, as well as a broad declarative knowledge, were very close to identifying the parameters better than the other participants at a significance level of $\alpha = 0.05$.

The gender difference observed can hardly be explained. The most probable explanation would be the constitution of the participants. Separately analyzed, women did not significantly differ from men with respect to a degree in music, profession, or the time span they were playing an instrument. But they were to a larger degree represented in several expertise groups. In sum, this might have had an effect in this particular case.

## 5.7 Summary

Listeners prefer eighth notes to be played inégal by different means. Surely, loudness, onset timing and tone duration are among these means. They are not independent from each other. In particular, loudness and timing are negatively correlated.

Participants with expert knowledge in Historically Informed Performance did not differ significantly from non-experts. But the data of participants who were able to identify the parameters by listening, showed a decreased variance. The difference in parameter identification between professional musicians and non-experts was, however, non-significant in most cases. But that the difference was near significance raises further questions that should be answered in future tests. Above all, the observation that professional musicians might differ from musicologists and skilled but nonprofessional performers led to the (still rather speculative) assumption, that expert knowledge comprises both, declarative knowledge and motor skill.

The technical challenge for this study was that the participants had to manipulate three parameters independently and interactively. By the use of an interactive tool, participants could adjust these three means in a four bar phrase taken from a piece of Baroque music. Besides the purely technical challenge, it was difficult for the participants to handle three parameters independently, especially for non-experts. A reason for this might be that humans tend to perceive—and as well produce—different performance parameters as one entirety of a musical movement.

**Acknowledgement** We thank all our participants from the Early Music Department of the Universität der Künste in Berlin, the "Zentrum für Telemann-Pflege und -Forschung Magdeburg", the Magdeburgian music school, the orchestra "Magdeburger Musikfreunde", the Otto-von-Guericke University Magdeburg, as well as those participants who do not belong to any of the above mentioned institutions.

## Bibliography

Austin, J. L. (1962), *How to do Things With Words. The William James Lectures delivered at Harvard University in 1955*, Oxford University Press, London.

Bengtsson, I. (1970), Studies with the Aid of Computers of "Music as Performed", *in* 'Report of the Tenth Congress, Ljubljana 1967', International Musicological Society, Bärenreiter, Kassel, pp. 443–444.

Bengtsson, I. & Gabrielsson, A. (1977), 'Rhythm research in Uppsala', *Music Room and Acoustics* pp. 19–56.

Berndt, A. (2010), Decentralizing Music, Its Performance, and Processing, *in* M. Schedel & D. Weymouth, eds, 'Proc. of the Int. Computer Music Conf. (ICMC)', International Computer Music Association, Stony Brook University, New York, USA, pp. 381–388.

Berndt, A. (2011*a*), Musical Tempo Curves, *in* M. Clarke, M. Adkins & B. Isaacs, eds, 'Proc. of the Int. Computer Music Conf. (ICMC)', International Computer Music Association, University of Huddersfield, Huddersfield, UK, pp. 118–121.

Berndt, A. (2011*b*), *Musik für interaktive Medien: Arrangement- und Interpretationstechniken*, Verlag Dr. Hut, Munich, Germany.

Berndt, A. & Hähnel, T. (2009), Expressive Musical Timing, *in* 'Audio Mostly 2009: 4th Conf. on Interaction with Sound—Sound and Emotion', Glasgow Caledonian University, Interactive Institute/Sonic Studio Piteå, Glasgow, Scotland, pp. 9–16.

Berndt, A. & Hähnel, T. (2010), Modelling musical dynamics, *in* 'Proc. of Audio Mostly: 5th Conf. on Interaction with Sound - Sound and Design', ACM, Piteå, pp. 134–141.

Butt, J. (2002), *Playing with History*, Cambridge University Press, Cambridge.

Clynes, M. & Walker, J. (1982), Neurobiological functions of rhythm, time, and pulse in music, *in* M. Clynes, ed., 'Music, Mind and Brain', New York, pp. 171–216.

Fabian, D. & Schubert, E. (2008), 'Musical Character and the performance and perception of dotting, articulation and tempo in 34 recordings of Variation 7 from J.S.Bach's Goldberg Variations (BWV 988)', *Musicae Scientiae* **12**(2), 177–206.

Friberg, A., Bresin, R. & Sundberg, J. (2006), 'Overview of the KTH Rule System for Musical Performance', *Advances in Cognitive Psychology, Special Issue on Music Performance* **2**(2–3), 145–161.

Gabrielsson, A. (1985), 'Interplay Between Analysis and Synthesis in Studies of Music Performance and Music Experience', *Music Perception* **3**(1), 59–86.

Gabrielsson, A. (1999), The Performance of Music, *in* D. Deutsch, ed., 'The Psychology of Music', Academic Press/Elsevier, San Diego, pp. 501–602.

Gerischer, C. (2003), *O singue baiano – Mikrorhythmische Phänomene in baianischer Perkussion*, Peter Lang, Frankfurt a.M., Germany.

Goebl, W. (2011), Die ungleichzeitige Gleichzeitigkeit des Spiels: Tempo rubato in Magaloff's Chopin und andere Asynchronizitäten, *in* H. von Loesch & S. Weinzierl, eds, 'Gemessene Interpretation: Computergestützte Aufführungsanalyse im Kreuzverhör der Disziplinen', TU Berlin, Schott Music, Mainz, Germany, chapter 10, pp. 145–156.

Hefling, S. E. (1993), *Rhythmic Alteration in Seventeenth- and Eighteenth-Century Music. Notes Inégales and Overdotting*, Schirmer Books, New York, NY.

Hähnel, T. (2010), From Mozart to MIDI: A Rule System for Expressive Articulation, *in* 'Proc. of New Interfaces for Musical Expression (NIME) 2010', University of Technology Sydney, Sydney, Australia, pp. 72–75.

Hähnel, T. (2013), *Baroque performance—a research study on characteristic parameters of 18th Century music*, Vol. 2 of *Studies in Cognitive Musicology*, Electronic Publishing Osnabrück, Osnabrück, Germany.

Hähnel, T. & Berndt, A. (2010), Expressive Articulation for Synthetic Music Performances, *in* 'Proc. of New Interfaces for Musical Expression (NIME) 2010', University of Technology Sydney, Sydney, Australia, pp. 277–282.

Hähnel, T. & Berndt, A. (2011*a*), Eighth-Notes Performances: Kinds of Inégalité, *in* 'Audio Mostly 2011: 6th Conf. on Interaction with Sound—Sound and Context', University of Coimbra, Interactive Institute/Sonic Studio Piteå, ACM SIGCHI, Coimbra, Portugal, pp. 75–81.

Hähnel, T. & Berndt, A. (2011*b*), Studying Interdependencies in Music Performance: An Interactive Tool, *in* 'Proc. of New Interfaces for Musical Expression (NIME) 2011', University of Oslo, Norwegian Academy of Music, Oslo, Norway, pp. 48–51.

Hinrichsen, H.-J. (2011), Kann Interpretation eine Geschichte haben? Überlegungen zu einer Historik der Interpretationsforschung, *in* H. v. Loesch & S. Weinzierl, eds, 'Gemessene Interpretation. Computergestützte Aufführungsanalyse im Kreuzverhör der Disziplinen.', Klang und Begriff 4, Schott, Berlin, pp. 27–39.

Hudson, R. (2004), *Stolen Time. The History of Tempo Rubato*, reprinted edn, Clarendon Press/Oxford University Press, Oxford, UK.

Langner, J. (2002), *Musikalische Rhythmen und Oszillation – Eine theoretische und empirische Erkundung*, Schriften zur Musikpsychologie und Musikästhetik - Band 13, Peter Lang, Frankfurt a.M.

Mazzola, G., Göller, S. & Müller, S. (2002), *The Topos of Music: Geometric Logic of Concepts, Theory, and Performance*, Birkhäuser Verlag, Zurich, Switzerland.

Metfessel, M. (1926), 'Sonance as a form of tonal fusion', *Psychological Review* **33**(6), 459–466.

MIDI Manufacturers Association (1996), The complete midi 1.0 detailed specification. v. 96.1, Technical report, MIDI Manufacturers Association, La Habra, CA.

Quantz, J. J. (1752), *Versuch einer Anweisung, die Flöte traversière zu spielen*, Bärenreiter. Reprint (1997), H. Augsbach.

Quantz, J. J. (2001), *On Playing the Flute. The Classic of Baroque Music Instruction*, Northeastern University Press, Berlin. Google Books. Second Edition. Translated with notes and an introduction by Edward R. Reilly. .

Seashore, H. (1932), The Hearing of the Pitch and Intensity in Vibrato, *in* C. E. Seashore, ed., 'The Vibrato', Vol. I of *Studies in the Psychology of Music*, University Press, Iowa, pp. 213–235.

Sevsay, E. (2005), *Handbuch der Instrumentationspraxis*, 1st edn, Bärenreiter, Kassel, Germany.

Shaffer, L. H. (1981), 'Performances of Chopin, Bach and Bartok: Studies in Motor Programming', *Cognitive Psychology* **13**, 326–376.

Speedsoft (2006), 'VSampler 3.5.2 Professional', http://www.vsampler3.com [last visited: Jan. 2010]. software sampler including a standard sample library.

Todd, N. P. (1985), 'A Model of Expressive Timing in Tonal Music', *Music Perception* **3**(1), 33–58.

Todd, N. P. (1989), 'A computational model of rubato', *Contemporary Music Review* **3**, 69–88.

Widmer, G., Flossmann, S. & Grachten, M. (2009), 'YQX Plays Chopin', *AI Magazine* **30**(3), 35–48.

Widmer, G. & Goebl, W. (2004), 'Computational Models of Expressive Music Performance: The State of the Art', *Journal of New Music Research* **33**(3), 203–216.

Felix Schönfeld

Chapter 6

# Vocalmetrics: Music Visualization and Rating Techniques

**Abstract** *Vocalmetrics* is a web application that provides scientific techniques for an interactive exploration and manipulation of multidimensional data. It was developed for the visualization and classification of musical data as a pivotal aim of music education and analysis. It introduces two visualization techniques: *Prototype Visualization,* as a very intuitive and playful way of exploring and classifying multidimensional musical data. *Egg Cell technique,* as a direct manipulative interaction technique for rating features of musical data, particularly suitable for subjective assessments.

## 6.1 Introduction

This chapter is based on the work of Schönfeld (2013), Schönfeld, Berndt, Hähnel, Pfleiderer & Groh (2014).

Music is ubiquitous and versatile and so is the perception of it. The classification of music helps to communicate about it, e.g. about its style, its time of creation and also about detailed musical features like structure, sound and expression. Therefore, the ability to classify music pieces and artists is a pivotal aim of music education. Ratings and classifications form an important basis for discussing and learning about musical characteristics, e.g. in classrooms or university seminars.

*Vocalmetrics* is a software tool that supports the communication about music. It has initially been developed as a visualization tool for musical data, in particular for analysed audio samples, which are an outcome of the research project *Voice and singing in popular music in the U.S.A (1900-1960)*[1] at the *Franz Liszt School of Music, Weimar*. These samples were rated according to nine dimensions of vocal expression in order to show relationships between song excerpts, singers, and their ratings. Since then the software has experienced further development, and the current version *Vocalmetrics 1.1*[2] offers the following functionalities:

- Geometric visualizations of multidimensional data (scatter plot, star plot)
- Similarity analysis between data records (*Prototype Visualization*)
- Supportive tool for rating data records (*Egg Cell Interaction Technique*)
- Multiple users and projects
- Data import/ export functionalities (from and to CSV-files)
- Web-based application

Section 2 looks at related work on visualizations of music in general, at similarity in general and at music similarity in particular.

The project's objectives are described in Section 3. As a first step, the data analysis and its consequences for the design concept of *Vocalmetrics* are outlined. Then, the software functionalities are described in detail starting with the general user interface and administration tools. The main part focuses on actual data visualizations and facilities to rate audio excerpts with the help of the *Prototype Visualization* and so-called *Egg Cell Interaction Technique*.

Finally, section 4 sheds light on spaces for improvements and points out implications of *Vocalmetrics* for musicological research and possible applications in music education.

Section 5 summarizes the chapter.

## 6.2 Related Work

The discipline of information visualization attempts to transform complex data into meaningful information by focussing on the human visual perception system. The data will be analysed and visualized by appropriate imaging techniques. Thus, the data can be viewed from different perspectives and new insights may be gained.

[1] `http://www.hfm-weimar.de/popvoices/vocalmetrics/main.htm`, last accessed: June 2015

[2] `http://schoenfelds.org/vocalmetrics`, last accessed: June 2015.

*Vocalmetrics* was developed to analyse multidimensional data. Suitable visualization techniques are differentiated into: *Geometric techniques*, which are summarized as a mapping of data features to attributes of the geometric space, e.g. *scatter plots* or *parallel coordinates*. It favours the visibility of specific data values, as these can be read accurately. *Iconic techniques* utilize the geometric space as well, but focus on one data object instead of the total quantity, e.g. *star plots*. The aim is to form a unique geometric figure for each data object based on its data features. This favours the interpretation of a data object as a whole and enables a comfortable comparison between different data objects. *Pixel-based techniques* try to map information to every single pixel of a presentation medium, to make full use of the available space and to avoid any white space. A common example are *Tree Maps*. (Schumann & Müller 2000)

Planetary[3] visualizes music collections with the help of a three-dimensional metaphor of the solar system. Artists are stars, surrounded by planets referring to their albums and those are surrounded by moons representing every single album track. A planet's texture is derived from the appearance of the album cover. The orbiting speed of the moons depends on the length of the track, and the size of the moons depends on the frequency of playbacks. The metaphor of the solar system is easy to understand and aesthetically well implemented, which has a positive effect on the user experience (UX). The universe as a three-dimensional information space invites the user to explore and interact. The approach can be assigned to the ZOIL (Zoomable Object-Oriented Information Landscape) paradigm (Jetter, König, Gerken & Reiterer 2008).

Dust & Magnet[4] is an information visualization system to support analysis and decision making for large and complex data sets with lots of variables. It uses the magnet metaphor to facilitate interpretation of multivariate data sets. Small circles (called dust) represent data items. Squares (called magnets) represent variables. As a magnet is dragged around on the screen, dust particles move towards it at different speeds. Data items with higher values for that magnet move faster. In other words they have a higher attraction with the magnet. With multiple magnets, dust particles are attracted to all of them simultaneously. Additionally, it is possible to map the circles' colour and size to a categorical or numerical variable respectively.

MusicGalaxy 2.0[5] visualizes music collections by mapping music titles as dots on a two-dimensional space (as stars in a galaxy). A star's position is calculated

[3] Bloom Studio Inc. (2011)
[4] Yi, Melton, Stasko & Jacko (2005)
[5] Stober & Nürnberger (2010)

with the help of LMDS (landmark-based multidimensional scaling), a technique for dimension reduction. Resulting projection errors are alleviated by an adaptive multifocal fisheye lens, i.e.: when focusing and distorting an area of interest with a fisheye lens (primary focus), a second fisheye lens automatically focuses on another area (secondary focus), whereby the second lens highlights music titles that are similar to music titles under the primary lens, but are positioned further away due to projection errors. The second fisheye lens alleviates the incorrect representation of spatial distance and similarity between data objects. The user can manipulate lots of parameters influencing the similarity calculation and the positioning of data items.

## 6.3 Concept & Development

The development process was accompanied by the research project *Voice and Singing* (see section 6.1), which delivered an example data set and served as a possible use scenario. From that perspective the application should allow the following tasks:

1. More visual exploration of research results as an alternative to looking at pure data tables
2. Direct listening to audio samples and providing access to additional information (e.g. spectrogram)
3. Uncovering of hidden patterns in the data set (e.g. outliers or similarities between data records) to gain new insights
4. Maintaining the data set (CRUD[6]) with efficient and error-resilient interaction techniques (integrated into the visualization itself)
5. User rating of features of data records (subjective feature assessment)
6. Supporting users to become familiar with different facets of the singing voice (educational purpose)

The process of rating data records as described in number 5 requires a closer inspection. As in the case of our example data set (see figure 6.1), there are general features that form a music title's meta information (artist, title etc.). Besides those, there are musical features that have to be evaluated, for example

[6]basic data operations: create, read, update, delete

by a music scientist, in consequence of his own subjective perception (vibrato, breathiness etc.). Therefore, features are categorized into objective and subjective features. Furthermore, a rating of a subjective feature can either be completely individual for the rating person (e.g. like or dislike) or a rating can claim to be generally valid as it is the case when experts have to compensate unavailable measuring instruments. The latter might suffer from interfering influences like perceptual disorders due to current mental conditions of the rating person or technical problems. The question is, how a software tool can support a person rating subjective features of data records, that are supposed to be generally valid. In order to promote general validity, the following thoughts might be worth considering during the rating process:

- Referring to and comparing with existing data records (reference frame)
- Adopting existent ratings (feature inheritance)
- Staying aware of the whole context and watch how a rating influences the data record's placement among existent records (e.g. direct manipulation)

### 6.3.1 Data Analysis

As a necessary task in data visualization, the data itself has to be analysed in detail to seek for the most fitting visualization approach. Looking at the example data set of the *Voice and Singing* project, there are over 200 data records, each having 15 features as shown in the data model (see figure 6.1). There is neither a hierarchy nor any linking between data records. The features can be split into objective and subjective features as described in the previous section. Subjective features are referred to as *ratable features* in the following. Objective features are rather categorical data types. The *release year* feature can also be used as quantitative (or continuous) data type. Ratable features are limited to a range of values from 0 to 100 and are therefore rather ordinal, but because of the large range, visualization techniques for quantitative data are probably more suitable in this case.

### 6.3.2 Visual Approach

The basic idea is to represent each data record as an independent visual object, to simplify matters, as a circle. The encoding of particular features is initially neglected. Applying this approach to the whole data set ends up in a chaotic point

| | feature | range of values | example |
|---|---|---|---|
| objective | artist | any text | Little Richard |
| | title | any text | rip it up |
| | gender | w / m | m |
| | label | any text | Specialty |
| | genre | any text | Rock'n'Roll |
| | release year | 1900 - 1960 | 1956 |
| subjective | **vibrato** | 0 - 100% | 0 |
| | **glissando** | 0 - 100% | 32 |
| | **intensity** | 0 - 100% | 67 |
| | **roughness** | 0 - 100% | 95 |
| | **breathiness** | 0 - 100% | 25 |
| | **register** | 0 - 100% | 31 |
| | **articulation** | 0 - 100% | 67 |
| | **rubato** | 0 - 100% | 8 |
| | **off-beat** | 0 - 100% | 58 |

**Figure 6.1:** Data model of the *Voice and Singing* project data.

cloud. It is assumed that every circle offers no more than a select-interaction to view its details. These conditions form the starting point for further design considerations. For a deeper exploration of the data set, the chaos needs to be organized with the help of additional interactions.

### 6.3.3 Administration And General User Interface

*Vocalmetrics* supports multiple projects and multiple users, which can be managed in the *Admin View* (see figure 6.2). A project is basically a container for an individual data set. An user is able to create a new project, define data features (dimensions), import prepared data records, start exploring the data set and do ratings for data records. Every user can give not more than one rating per data record. A data record can have multiple ratings by different users. The possibility of multiple users enables a comparison between the subjective perception of different raters and derives a generally valid rating using statistical methods such as the average calculation.

The design of *Vocalmetrics* is intended to be as non-distractive as possible to keep the focus on the actual data visualizations. The upper area of the screen holds the details area (see figure 6.3), which shows the feature values of the selected data records. The upper right corner holds the audio player, which can play back an attached audio file of a data record. The lower left corner contains the

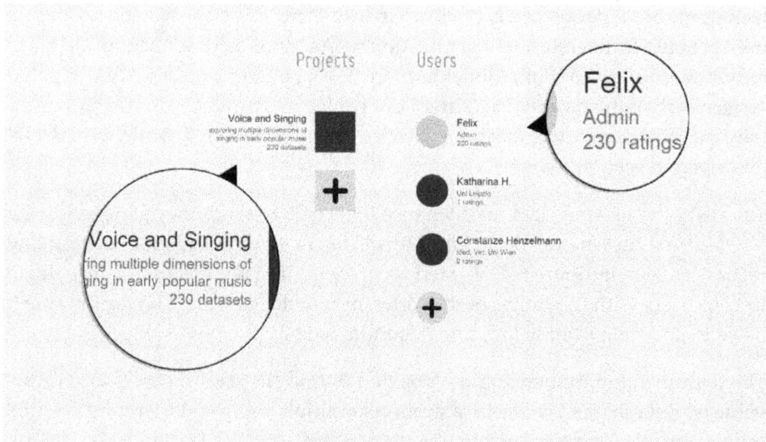


**Figure 6.2:** The admin view.

view menu, where the user can switch between different views representing the individual visualizations. In the lower center there is a text box for searching for certain data records. The right edge of the screen offers additional view functionalities, where some are available only in certain views. Via a grid, the user can change the colour scheme from dark to bright or add new data records. The center of the screen holds the actual data visualization of the current view. Yellow circles are currently selected by the user; a multiple selection is possible. Data records can be selected in order to show their details or to highlight them, which makes it easier to follow when applying visual changes. Circles with a red outline are matching the search criteria the user typed into the search box.

### 6.3.4 Basic Visualizations And Interactions

The *Scatter Plot View* (see figure 6.3) implements a basic scatter plot visualization and enriches it with additional functionalities. It offers a Cartesian coordinate system to position data records based on two of their feature values. Besides the X and Y coordinates, there are two more visual variables available to be mapped to other features: size of the circle and its opacity. The mapping of visual variables and features can be changed by the user at any time, whereas the visual impacts are applied with a motion transition supporting a better understanding of coherences. The perception and tracking of changes can be assisted by selecting multiple data records (yellow circles). With this basic functionalities the user benefits from common visualization interactions as described in the *Visual Information-Seeking Mantra* (Shneiderman 1996), i.e. it enables the user to get an "overview" of the data set, to "filter" out irrelevant data records and show "details" of records of interest. This solves the tasks number 1, 2, 3 and 6 on the list described in section 6.3.

To satisfy the need of data maintenance tools (see task number 5 in section 6.3) *Vocalmetrics* implements basic input forms to create new and edit existing data records as seen in figure 6.4. The left form for editing data records offers sliders to help users with the rating of the different ratable features. The user is able to listen to an audio sample and rate it simultaneously.

The feature value influencing the position within the scatter plot is an average value by default. As *Vocalmetrics* supports multiple users and therefore multiple ratings per data record, a value of a data record's ratable feature is, by default, the calculated average of all ratings, that users have made for this individual data record. This behaviour can be changed by the user: it is possible to specify a subset of users, which causes the visualization to be influenced only by ratings of those users. This way individual ratings can be compared more detailed. This function is important, because on the one hand, the average calculation of multiple ratings can ensure the overall validity, but on the other hand, it is not possible to determine whether the individual user ratings are similar or differ strongly, e.g. to find out which features are rated reliably or where users do not act well as an alternative to technical measurements.

### 6.3.5 Prototype Visualization

Assuming that the user seeks for a specific subset of data records, his mental picture contains certain criteria, which he uses to focus on certain data records, he assigns them to a certain category or class respectively. The user would compare data records among themselves and determine their similarity or dissimilarity concerning his criteria. This requires the user to have a concrete imagination about his criteria. Data visualization often serves as a helping hand in the search for new insights, so users might not have concrete ideas about what they look for. In order to support the user in this case, the *Prototype Theory* formulated by Rosch (1983) can help. Conventionally, classes within a classification system can be separated clearly from each other by defining fixed rules about which elements fit and which do not fit in a specific class. With prototypes, the transitions

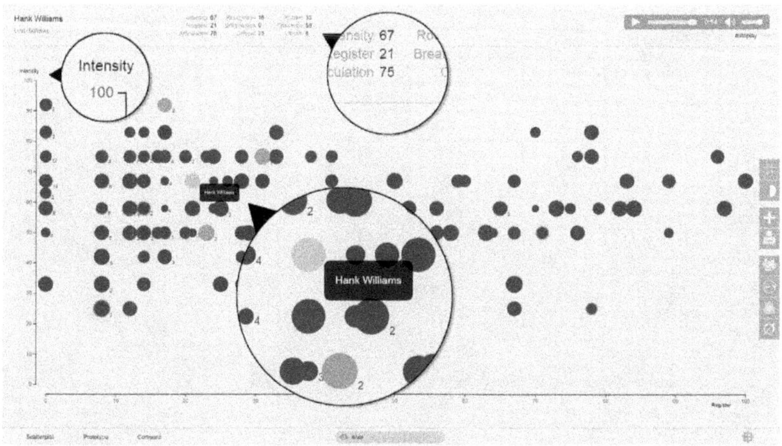


**Figure 6.3:** The Scatter Plot View.

between classes become smooth. A prototype defines a class as a typical representative of certain characteristics. Any record within the data set can serve as a prototype. Data records then have a gradual belonging to this class based on their similarity with the prototype. In fact, every data record belongs to this class, because every record has a calculable similarity to the prototype. This way, the user does not have to define fixed rules when organizing a data set with the help of a classification system.

The *Prototype Theory* is applied as *Prototype Visualization* (see figure 6.5). The similarity between data records or between a prototype and other records respectively is calculated based on the *Euclidean Distance* using the $n$ ratable features as dimensions of an $n$-dimensional vector. The visual implementation uses a magnet metaphor, i.e. data records get attracted by prototypes and move towards them until a certain distance is reached, which represents its calculated similarity to the prototype. As seen in figure 6.5, gray circles are unorganized data records and form the "chaos" as mentioned in section 6.3.2. The blueish circles are data records, that were transformed into a prototype. White circles are attracted by prototypes and spatially positioned according to their similarity with the prototype, which is additionally visualized by the linking lines and their thickness. In contrast to the theoretical background in the previous paragraph, not all data records are attracted by a prototype although they have a calculable distance to it. An adjustable distance limit was established, enabling the user to

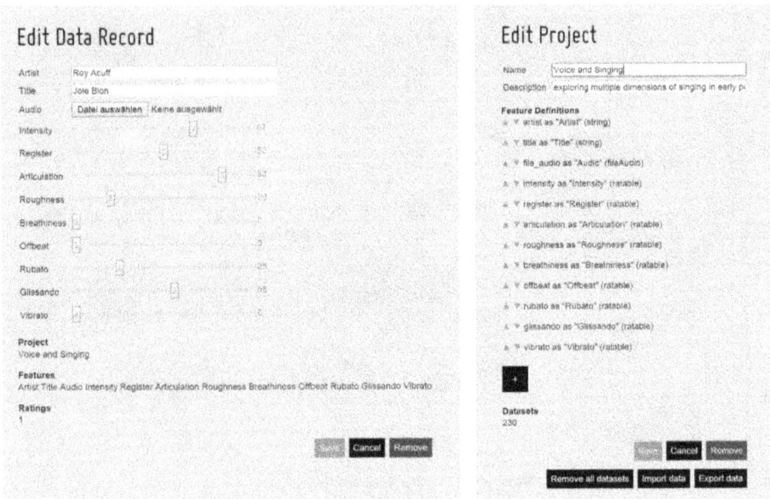


**Figure 6.4:** Input forms for basic data operations (CRUD).

focus on data records that have a minimum similarity to the created prototype. Therefore, all data records that exceed the distance limit, are not attracted. Due to the fact, that data records are basically attracted by every prototype except they exceed the distance limit, some data records still belong to more than one prototype. This is visualized by multiple linking lines between a data record and each prototype attracting it. All objects can be freely arranged with the help of drag and drop interactions.

### 6.3.6 Egg Cell Technique

As seen in section 6.3.4 the data input forms allow the user to rate data records with the help of sliders. Section 6.3 also points out the requirement for an alternative, more visual rating process supporting the user to rate reliably and ensure the general validity of ratings within the data set. The application of the three mentioned proposals from section 6.3 will be described in the following.

Figure 6.6 demonstrates the concept of a rating tool using direct manipulative interactions, called *Egg Cell Interaction Technique*. It is integrated within the *Prototype View* (see section 6.3.5). The nine green prototypes (*pure prototypes*) are

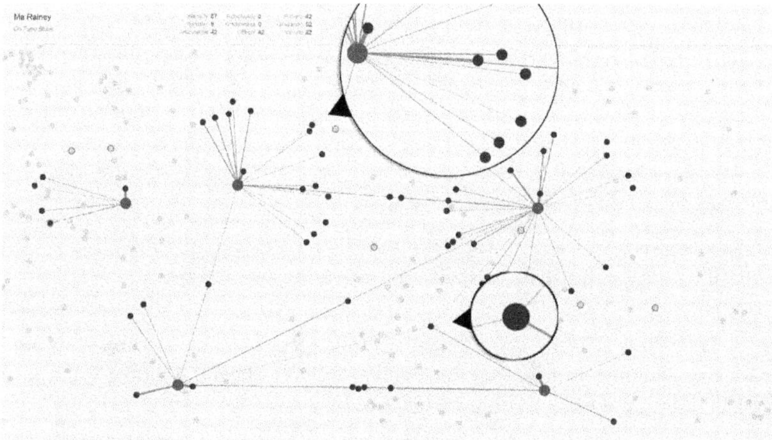


**Figure 6.5:** The Prototype View.

created automatically and can be used only within the rating process. They are referred to as *pure* because each of them represents one of the ratable features exclusively and these prototypes are not based on an existing data record. They serve as circularly arranged sliders with their dragging direction orientated towards the center. Pure prototypes also attract typical representatives of one specific feature that can be used for comparative listening. Its visualization consists of the *cell nucleus* (red circle in the center), the *cell envelope* and the *sperms* (other existing data records and prototypes). The data record to be rated is represented by the cell nucleus, but also as a red circle among the other data records in the space. In contrast to the rating process that uses sliders in the input forms, where feature values are *directly* given by the user, this technique can be used for an *indirect* rating. The user rates indirectly by referring to other data records and indicates relations between those and the data record that is to be rated.

The user would rate a data record by starting the rating process inside the *Prototype View* and listening to the attached audio sample of the data record to be rated. Optionally other data records can be used for comparative listening. Then the user sets the features of a data record (cell nucleus) by moving existing data records (sperms) into the area of inheritance (within the cell envelope). The closer a data object is moved towards the cell nucleus, the more the cell nucleus inherits the data object's feature values. The resulting feature values of the rated data record are combined inheritances from user-created prototypes and pure prototypes. It performs an interpolation of the features of all objects within the cell envelope, by their distance to the core. However, a green pure prototype inside the cell envelope dominates the rating of its particular dimension and causes the value of all other data objects to be ignored. Thus, it defines an absolute value for its respective feature solely. The influence on the rated data record can be observed immediately with the help of the smaller pink circle, which is the data record that is currently rated.

The concept has further improvements and interaction patterns. So far, it supports the rating of musical data with the following advantages:

- The whole data set is present. Each data record can be used for comparative listening and can be referenced to actively affect the rating. Change of a rating immediately changes the visual state of the rated data record.
- The use of prototype semantics allows for a weighted inheritance of feature values. This facilitates the rating, because similar audio samples can be adopted and complex feature combinations are applied much quicker than by rating each feature individually. Moreover, prototype semantics automatically provides reference pieces for comparative listening.
- Direct input of numeric values is possible, but largely avoided. For questions like „What is a maximum vibrato?"or „When is it medium?", absolute values are inappropriate. Instead, the focus lies on a more relational rating which complies better with the object of analysis, music.
- The slider-like dragging of objects closer to the core reflects an intuitive direct relation of proximity and similarity.

## 6.4 Discussion

*Vocalmetrics* has not been officially evaluated yet. Experiences among musicologists show, that common tasks in musical research projects can be optimized when using *Vocalmetrics*, especially the presentation and exploration of research data as well as the process of data creation or gathering respectively. *Vocalmetrics* combines both tasks in one application.

The *Scatter Plot View* enriches a well-known visualization technique with useful functionality, which is gladly accepted by the user. The *Prototype Visualization*

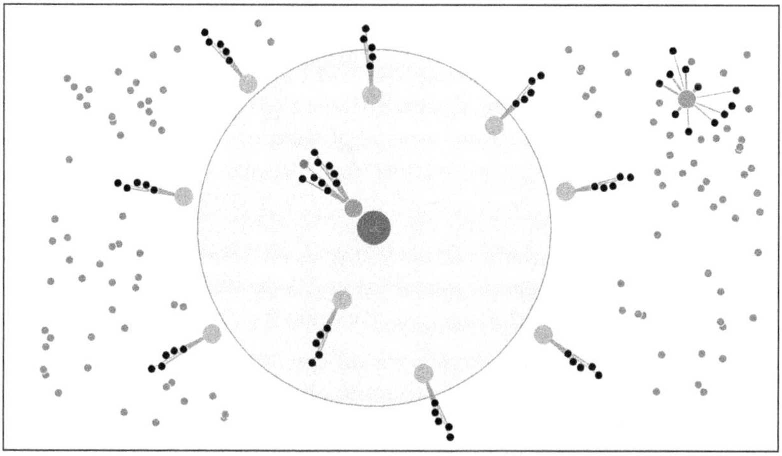

**Figure 6.6:** Concept of the Egg Cell Technique as a supportive rating tool.

and its strong agility of lively moving circles can be very comfortable to interact with. However, the logical connections beyond can be hard to understand. On the one hand, it is an easily understandable tool for finding similar objects visualized by their geometric distances and the magnet metaphor. On the other hand, the user can quickly create a very complex graph structure with $n$-to-$m$ relations which are hard to differentiate and understand clearly. The *Prototype Visualization* resembles the *Dust & Magnet* software (Yi et al. 2005). It was developed independently and emerged as an exemplary implementation of the prototype theory. Our model further includes a distance constraint which is added to the physical model. This causes attracted objects not to move towards the magnetic object as close as possible, but to stop at a certain distance depending on their similarity. The similarity-distance-relation can not generally be guaranteed, which is inherent to every dimension reduction method. Therefore, the introduced *Prototype Visualization* does not reflect the complex similarity relations among all data records. Nevertheless, it can serve as an alternative to other techniques for visualizing similarity, like dimension reduction, which is accompanied by projection errors and also requires the user to have advanced skills for an useful understanding.

The same data visualization that is used to represent the research data, can be used to manipulate the data. Results are shown immediately. There is no need of external data maintenance. When dealing with data containing subjective attributes, that have to be evaluated by a capable person, the supportive rating tools of *Vocalmetrics* can help. Creating new datasets within the visualizations itself is very useful. The instant feedback of how a newly added data record will be positioned among the existing amount of records is easily comprehensible and leads to a very positive user experience. Users experience an improvement of the rating process and appreciate the comfort of listening and rating simultaneously. It enables the user to stay focused on the actual task of rating a musical piece and increases the user's motivation to keep on working. The minimal design supports a distraction-free interaction and perception process. The visual focus lies on the data rather than on auxiliary functionalities.

The combination of *Prototype Visualization* and *Egg Cell Interaction Technique* helps users to benefit from their individual classification of a music repertoire, when rating new audio samples to expand the repertoire. They can classify new audio samples according to their own classification methods, as represented by the prototypes they create and then use for adaptation. However, the result can be a complex set of inheriting objects inside the cell envelope. It therefore needs further decisions concerning inheritance dominances. Also the interplay of direct and indirect attribution should be improved towards a better handling and user experience, i.e., the balance of direct numeric input of feature values and the indirect adaptation by means of inheritance.

Users can easily create and manage new projects choosing individual audio samples and any rating and meta data dimensions. Ratings and meta data can be exported for further statistical analysis. The data could serve as a starting point for various research issues, e.g. how individuals listen to music and how effects of music on emotion and mood differ between individual listeners. Therefore, Vocalmetrics can serve as a valuable data collection tool for research in music psychology and music pedagogy. *Vocalmetrics* furthermore provides techniques that are suitable also for non-musical, multidimensional data. *Vocalmetrics* is a tool for visualization and comfortable maintenance of multidimensional data. Users benefit from this application as a quick and easy to use analysis tool for data of their interest.

## 6.5 Conclusions

*Vocalmetrics v1.1* offers many valuable possibilities to visualize similarities and differences between music pieces or audio samples relating to various features of musical structure, sound, and performance as well as relating to meta data. On the one hand, *Vocalmetrics* can help to classify, explore, and compare large repertoires of music and music of differing provenience. On the other hand, it offers a quick and intuitive approach for visualizing features of and relations between music excerpts and, hence, to communicate about music in various settings. Listeners reflect on these features and relations during the rating process which might also exert an educational gain.

The chapter describes *Vocalmetrics* as a software tool for data visualization and manipulation. It introduces the *Prototype Visualization* as an intuitive and playful way of exploring complex data sets and analysing similarities and differences between data records. Furthermore, it offers tools for the process of rating subjective data attributes such as musical features that are assessed by music experts. Therefore, the *Egg Cell Interaction Technique* is introduced as a tool for indirect rating, i.e. to set the values of data features by referring to and adopting from other data records instead of specifying a feature value directly by numerical input.

Section 6.1 gives a quick introduction of a musical research project called *Voice and Singing*, which was the occasion to develop the software. Section 6.2 looks at related work in the field of music similarity visualizations. The project objectives and software requirements are described in Section 6.3, followed by the data analysis and its consequences for the design concept of *Vocalmetrics*. Then, the software functionalities and visualizations are described in detail. Section 6.4 mentions experienced problems and possible improvements of the *Vocalmetrics* software as well as its benefits for musical research and education.

## Bibliography


Bloom Studio Inc. (2011), 'Planetary'. a visual music player for iPad.
**URL:** *http://planetary.bloom.io*

Jetter, H.-C., König, W. A., Gerken, J. & Reiterer, H. (2008), ZOIL—A Cross-Platform User Interface Paradigm for Personal Information Management, *in* 'Proc. of the CHI 2008 Workshop on Personal Information Management (PIM 2008)', Florence, Italy.

Rosch, E. (1983), Prototype Classification and Logical Classification: The Two Systems, *in* E. K. Scholnick, ed., 'New Trends in Conceptual Representation: Challenges to Piaget's Theory?', Taylor & Francis, chapter 3, pp. 73–86.

Schönfeld, F. (2013), Entwicklung eines Rating-Tools für die Erstellung musikwissenschaftlicher Datensätze, student research project, Technische Universität Dresden, Faculty of Computer Science, Dresden, Germany.

Schönfeld, F., Berndt, A., Hähnel, T., Pfleiderer, M. & Groh, R. (2014), Vocalmetrics: An interactive software for visualization and classification of music, *in* 'Audio Mostly 2014: 9th Conf. on Interaction with Sound—Imagining Sound and Music', Aalborg University, Interactive Institute/Sonic Studio Piteå, ACM, Aalborg, Denmark.

Schumann, H. & Müller, W. (2000), *Visualisierung: Grundlagen und allgemeine Methoden*, Springer, Berlin, Heidelberg, Germany.

Shneiderman, B. (1996), The Eyes Have It: A Task by Data Type Taxonomy for Information Visualizations, *in* 'IEEE Symposium on Visual Languages', Boulder, CO, USA, pp. 336–343.

Stober, S. & Nürnberger, A. (2010), MusicGalaxy—An Adaptive User-Interface for Exploratory Music Retrieval, *in* 'Proc. of the 7th Sound and Music Computing Conf. (SMC)', University Pompeu Fabra, Barcelona, Spain, pp. 382–389.

Yi, J. S., Melton, R., Stasko, J. & Jacko, J. A. (2005), 'Dust & magnet: multivariate information visualization using a magnet metaphor', *Information Visualization* **4**(4), 239–256.

# Index